THE EAGLE AND THE BEAR

The Philosophic Roots of

Democracy and Communism

Pennington Haile

The Eagle and the Bear

THE PHILOSOPHIC ROOTS OF
DEMOCRACY AND COMMUNISM

AN IVES WASHBURN BOOK

DAVID McKAY COMPANY, INC. · NEW YORK

THE EAGLE AND THE BEAR:
THE PHILOSOPHIC ROOTS OF DEMOCRACY AND COMMUNISM

COPYRIGHT 1950 BY PENNINGTON HAILE
COPYRIGHT © 1965 BY PENNINGTON HAILE

SECOND EDITION REVISED 1965

LIBRARY OF CONGRESS CATALOG CARD NUMBER: 64–16120

MANUFACTURED IN THE UNITED STATES OF AMERICA

Foreword

FOR WHATEVER merit this brief inquiry may possess, I am deeply indebted to an earlier work, *The Meeting of East and West,* by F. S. C. Northrop of Yale University.

When I first read that illuminating book, I felt very strongly that its chapters on the differing philosophic roots which have nourished the development of the United States and the Soviet Union set forth ideas of the greatest importance. I was sure that these ideas cast a new and clarifying light on the world scene of today, and I felt it to be essential that they be separated from the wealth of other material in Professor Northrop's work, and be brought into sharper focus with reference to current problems.

Developments since that time have served only to increase the need for wider understanding of these same ideas. We cannot comprehend, much less control, the conflict between our nation and Soviet Russia unless we look back into the wellsprings out of which have been drawn their opposing ways of life.

As the years of the cold war continue I believe that we in this country are handicapped by insufficient understanding of our own deepest roots of thought. We need to understand not only the present political and economic features of the differences between democratic and totalitarian society but also the causes of those differences. For they did not just happen to develop differently. There were very important reasons why their respective developments took the directions they did. The nature of their roots determined the character of their growth. There is great need for us to probe these roots if we are to meet successfully the challenges we face. We need not only to uncover our philosophic heritage but also to ask ourselves if our present policies square with it. We need also to comprehend the very different roots from which the systems of those who oppose us have grown. Knowledge of our own bases of thought is essential for self-understanding and for the shaping of an intelligent and consistent foreign policy. Knowledge of the bases of Communist thought is equally important if we are to combat successfully Communist policies and propaganda.

In the current struggle that divides our world it is of paramount importance to arm our *minds* if we are to prevail. Our adversaries have so far done a better job than we in teaching those who spread their gospel, its origins, and its development. Often they outdo us for this very reason. The world today is hungry for better ideas as a vital part of a better life. All too often it has seemed that the Communists win out because their ideas seem new and fresh, ours old and stale. To disprove this is of primary importance. How well will our ideas of the relation of man and state serve us—and the rest of mankind? In what ways do they need to be amended—if in any? These are questions we cannot evade, and the burden of answering them rests upon us now as never before. For no amount of military or material might will win us friends or favor for long unless based on acceptable concepts of man and of the state.

It is my modest hope that this inquiry may help us to discover an inner confidence without which no outer show of strength will suffice.

Pennington Haile

September, 1964

Contents

THE EAGLE AND THE BEAR

The Philosophic Roots of

Democracy and Communism

1

The Basis of Conflict

A S THIS is written, the United States and the Soviet Union, two great giants in a world grown small, walk about each other and measure each other's strength, like two fighters in a ring.

That ring is the world itself; the stakes are life and death. No longer are we the only contestants; China ranks as a rival Communist power, France dissolves the unity of the West. But the policies of Washington and Moscow are still the main weights in the scales of war and peace.

All of us, all the men and women of the world, we who have so much to gain by peace and to lose by war, must ask ourselves constantly, "Is there any way, as yet untried, in which we can seek deeper understanding of the reasons for existence of that chasm which today splits the power and the thought of our world? Can we, in any way, comprehend more fully why we of the West believe, and react, and live as we do, why the Russians believe, and react as they do?"

I think that there is such a way, and that we shall be better citizens of our land, and of the world, for exploring it. So far, few have ventured into it; it is time for us all to do so. It is the approach to understanding offered by the study of the relatively few, great, basic ideas that underlie our system, and that of Soviet Russia. These ideas are not political or economic in their nature; they are truly philosophical, for they deal with man's basic concepts about his own nature.

That it is time for us to investigate these ideas is clear. Often we ask ourselves why we believe in the sort of political and social system under which we live, and why we fear other systems. We need assurance as to the validity of our ways, and of our values. We are prepared to admit that these ways, these values, are not perfect. But we are very sure that they still offer more to men than do any others. Sometimes, however, we are not quite sure enough. At such times we falter and fumble although the world needs our leadership now as never before.

It is when men forget the fundamental ideas on the basis of which their political and social forms are built that the drive goes out of their society. It is hard for a nation to give moral as well as material leadership—as we must do today—if its people do not remember the foundation of their faith, or the logical ground for their political and social institutions. It is hard for a nation to cope with a powerful rival if it does not understand the bases on which that rival has developed its own differing sort of society. We must, therefore, explore the ideas out of which the United States and the Soviet Union have shaped their present ways of life.

You cannot discover these ideas merely by looking at the form of political organization of each nation. Much less can you find them by examining only the attitudes and prejudices of their inhabitants. Indeed, they will not even be revealed by studying the text of their Constitutions, although in these texts their application may be found. No, you must go deeper still into the heritage of thought which shaped the development of the United States and the Soviet Union if you want full understanding of their political and social organization, of the patterns of behavior of their peoples, and of the dangerous tension that exists between them.

One chief trouble with our cleft earth today is that we do not probe deeply enough the reasons for its cleavage. We compare and contrast the institutions and characteristics of each part; we do not ask ourselves why and how the differences have developed between them.

Why, for example, do we of the United States believe in the primary importance of freedom of religion, and of thought, and of speech? Why do we so admire individual initiative, and dislike any but the most necessary interference by government in our affairs? These characteristics did not just happen to develop. Nor did it come about by chance that the citizens of the Soviet Union have been far more willing than we to submit their individual wills, opinions, and activities to the control of the state.

We have seen already that our inquiry is going to lead us into the cloudy realm of philosophy. To many of us, philosophy may seem a remote and impractical field. Yet it represents an activity as natural to man as the search for food and love. Man, like all creatures, must eat and breed. But, unlike all others, he must also *know*. Philosophy is the story of man's attempt to know the basic nature of himself, and of his world. As philosopher, man perennially asks himself such questions as: "What is the world really like in its true nature? It is a mechanical, meaningless world, or is there a purpose, a goal, a God in it?" And he asks: "What am I really like? Am I, as a thinking, self-conscious being, different from other creatures? Does my presence in the world mean anything special? Can I know anything more than what my senses tell me? What is my essential nature, my proper function?"

On the basis of answers which satisfy him for the time being, man forms his ideas as to his own nature. In accordance with such ideas he develops his theories about society and govern-

ment. What man conceives his own nature and proper function
to be determines the political and social forms under which
he desires to live. This fact is the reason for this present inquiry.

Were we to search through all the pages of history, we
should find that only a few concepts as to man's nature and
proper function have been compelling enough to shape men's
thoughts, or to mold the sort of society formed to accord with
them. The scope of this present study will be far more modest,
but we shall never fully understand, let alone resolve, the conflict that exists between us and the Russians until we can
comprehend how utterly different our traditional idea of the
nature and function of man is from theirs.

Such matters may seem remote from the immediate problem
of the day-to-day tension that threatens our world. It shall be
our purpose to show that they are not at all remote; indeed,
that the tension can be relieved only if we understand them.

To comprehend the contrast between democratic and totalitarian forms of society we need to dig into the philosophic
subsoil of both, as a gardener must analyze the different sorts
of soil in order to understand the growth of flowers and weeds
that spring from each.

Of course, our inquiry will not clear up entirely the mis-
understandings that exist or, much less, heal the division of
our fearful earth. But it can, at least, explain a great deal that
puzzles and irritates us. It can, for example, give us a better
understanding of ourselves. It can show how we and the
Russians both use the words freedom and democracy and yet
mean entirely different things. It can explain why conferences
with Russia, inside or outside of the United Nations, are almost
surely doomed to failure. It can make clear why every Russian
diplomat merely repeats the statements issued by The Party.
It can explain in large measure what the really dangerous
elements are in Russia's policy and program. It can give us a
better basis for a consistent foreign policy. It can set forth for

us, and for all the world, the basis for such a policy in our own philosophic heritage.

To do all this certainly sets us a challenge. But, before we try to meet it, we should remind ourselves of two things. First, we must remember that both the United States and the Soviet Union were established as the result of revolution. This, of course, we well know. But we may not realize that in each case the revolution involved was more than a rebellion against the regime which had preceded it. Each was a revolution in a profound, philosophic sense as well as in a political way. Ours was not aimed merely at the England of George III; it was a revolt against the whole tradition of medieval society. The Bolshevik revolution of 1917 was not aimed merely at the Kerensky government which had overthrown the Czar. It was a revolt against the whole western tradition of a "free society."

Second, we must always keep in mind that the United States and the Soviet Union represent the embodiment of two different concepts of the Ideal State, two differing visions of Utopia. Whatever our weaknesses may be, whatever the glaring faults of Russia, both nations represent to millions of their own people, and to many elsewhere, an attempt to realize a vision of a better life for man. We know this is true of our own land. We should realize too that, despite its obvious betrayal of so much of the hope that gave it birth, the Soviet Union still holds the allegiance of many who once saw in it the projection of such a dream.

For, within the historic span of the Christian Era, western man has lived by the light of three great visions. First, the sustaining dream of the dark medieval period, in which man's hopes were centered in heaven, his fears in hell.

In revolt against this, with the "Age of Enlightenment," came the bright, exciting vision of a society founded on personal freedom. In such a society, man, guided by the light of reason, and freed from any pre-ordained authority of church or state, could decide on the amount and kind of political control

needed to protect his freedom. Out of this dream was shaped
the United States of America.

Later, there came a third vision, born out of the suffering
and disillusionment of millions whom the dream of freedom
seemed to have betrayed. This was the dream of a life of
security underwritten by the state for the well-being of a classless society. This was the genesis of the Soviet Union.

Today the two later dreams of man, embodied in the two
most powerful states of our earth, are, to a large extent, the
leaven of the conflict between them.

Our main task will be to examine the basic concepts as to
the nature and function of man which undergird the political
and social organization of our nation, and of the Soviet Union.
But the history of man's hopes requires that we trace the development of the three guiding dreams which have engendered
medieval and modern societies. First, we must recall the chief
concepts that were the basis for that medieval world against
which our own revolution was directed, and the last vestiges of
which it tried to sweep away.

2

The Medieval
View of Man

SO NOW we must turn back to the world picture which mankind accepted during the middle ages. In doing so, we shall have to recount, in as short and simple a form as possible, the philosophic bases on which that picture rested. It may seem strange to many that we have to go back that far in order to characterize the sort of world against which the Declaration of Independence was aimed. The world of 1776 was certainly not that of the middle ages. But the old and outworn ideas as to how society should be organized, those very ideas against which the Declaration was a revolt, were still medieval in their approach to the nature of the world, of man, and of society. Therefore, it is necessary to go far back into the history of human thought in order to make clear what sort of world picture it was against which the fundamental ideas of the American Revolution were directed.

We know that during the middle ages whatever light of knowledge burned was cared for, and guarded by, the Church of Rome. It was the Fathers of the Church, the so-called "Scholastics," who carried on most of whatever philosophical speculation there was during the long centuries of that era. We may have forgotten, however, that the medieval era extended over a thousand years, almost twice as many centuries as the modern world has as yet endured. No wonder that the conditioning given to the thought and literature of the western world by the medieval period still provides much of the background for the modern mind.

Most of us are aware that during all the medieval period it was to the Church that men looked for knowledge as to the nature of the world, as well as for instruction as to the approaches to heaven. But we do not, perhaps, all realize that the hold which the Church had over men's hearts and minds during the middle ages was not based merely on superstitious awe and the fear of hell. These elements played an important role, as they always have in almost wholly illiterate societies. But the Church could also command allegiance of the intellect of the educated few. It could do so because its doctrines and dogmas were founded on a complete and rational world picture which was entirely satisfactory according to the science and philosophy of the time. It is with this philosophic background of the medieval world picture that we are concerned. For only when it collapsed was the transition from the medieval to the modern world possible.

Since the Church of Rome so dominated the medieval scene, it is with the philosophic bases of Christianity that we must deal. All great religions, Christianity among them, command the passionate allegiance of their believers because they teach, in simple and dramatic form, a way of life that men for some reason want to follow. The Christian way of life appeals to many of man's finer, gentler instincts, and promises, either in this world or the next, a better life. In the case of Christianity this emotional appeal has, almost from its origin, been supplemented by the intellectual appeal of a supporting system of philosophy.

It is generally agreed that the philosophic background for the teachings of the medieval church came from Greece. It is probably right to say that this background was at first drawn from Plato. Certainly, St. Augustine, the greatest of the early Fathers, was steeped in Plato's thought about the nature of the world. Here, we need to be concerned only with one element in Plato's thinking. He believed that there are two different "worlds," one which we know through our senses, one which we apprehend with our reason. The first is imperfect and transitory; the second, perfect and eternal. The first we see, hear, taste, and smell; the second we "see" only with the "mind's eye." Here, we are already in touch with one of the permanent problems of philosophy—can we know anything more of the world than the stream of impressions which our senses give us? We shall see how this problem haunts the systems of thought which we must investigate in our seach for the philosophic roots of our political and social theories, and those of Russia.

For Plato, the "other world," that of the mind, was more real than the world of sense impressions. In the latter we experience imperfect examples of beauty, of justice, of friendship, of love. But, in the world which we know only through our reason, we come to know the perfect forms, the very "Ideas," as Plato called them, of Beauty, Justice, Friendship, Love.

One can easily see how the early Church Fathers found in this doctrine of Plato's a philosophic basis for proclaiming that there was a Kingdom of Heaven, perfect and permanent, and a Kingdom of This World, filled with error and illusion. Thus a philosophic background out of the rich heritage of Greek thought was found for the doctrines of the medieval Church. This was grafted on to its teachings as to how a man could pass from the sorrows of this world to the joys and rewards of heaven. This was not only a tribute to the power and persuasion of Plato's thought, but also to the perennial conviction of man that his mind can voyage beyond the shores of sense.

Plato had never very satisfactorily shown how the world of sense and the world of "Ideas" were related. As a result, his philosophy seemed to some unsatisfactory as a basis for explaining the relation of the Kingdom of Heaven to that of this world. But, in the thirteenth century, a new philosophic basis for the teachings of medieval Christendom was found in the writings of Aristotle, whose works had by then been rediscovered. They had been restored through the growing influence of Arabic scholars, who had preserved many of them through all the long dissolution of the Roman world. As the tide of the invasion of the "Moors" swept westward and northward, this heritage of learning which their wise men had preserved began to permeate the whole Christian world.

We cannot possibly deal with all the reasons why the Church shifted the philosophic setting of its doctrines from Plato to Aristotle. Many of them had to do with the better basis which the latter's world picture gave for mathematics and physics. We are concerned only with the better basis given for "metaphysics," as Aristotle himself called it—that which lies beyond physics. We can deal with this only as it affected the background for the world picture of the medieval Church.

Unlike Plato, Aristotle believed that the world we know through our senses is itself the "real" world. For him, there was not the sharp division between the world as known by man's senses and the world as conceived by his reason. This does not mean that Aristotle thought that the world we see and hear and taste was all there was to "Reality." For no one in the history of human thought has ever believed more utterly in a basic Purpose in the world. This purpose, this design, this "God," if you will, was within all things. This element, Aristotle called the "form" of each thing. This form, this purposeful element, had to work through matter which was inert, even "reluctant," and so "form" could never perfectly fulfill itself.

For Aristotle, all things were graded according to the degree that each could realize its own indwelling purpose. Inorganic matter could do so very imperfectly, living things far better. But man, as a conscious being, could do so best of all. Furthermore, a man's "soul," the purposeful element within him, was itself conscious of its purpose. Thus man has a "moral" responsibility for realizing the best that is within him which animals do not share.

Thomas Aquinas, a priest and student of Christian theory, had long pored over the philosophy of Aristotle. Finally, in his massive *Summa Theologica,* he had perfected its implications so that they might serve as a new and better philosophic basis for the Christian world picture. Nor is it hard to see how he could do so convincingly. For him, and for the world picture which he painted, all things, from acorns to archbishops, were graded in a sort of ascending hierarchy. From polyp to Pope there ran a chain of ascending excellence according to the degree which each classification could attain of realizing its own inner "form."

In this view there was a purposefulness in all things, and this in its own nature was identifiable with God. Thus the Kingdom of God was not remote from, and unrelated to, that of this world. Instead, the former was constantly and wonderfully revealing itself in the latter. All things showed in varying degrees this revelation of purpose. Man could understand this, and himself aid in its development. In so far as this purposefulness could be grasped by man's limited intelligence, it could be comprehended by reason. In so far as it could not be, it must be approached through faith and accepted as revelation. Learned men could use reason where the illiterate must depend upon faith. And the Church, which at the time was the stronghold of reason as well as the arbiter of revelation, saw itself as the proper authority to assess the relative value of all things and all men, and to interpret the purposes of God.

It is easy to see how this view lent itself to a concept of the world as a sort of hierarchy of graded forms, rising from inorganic things through living creatures to human beings.

We should note that Aristotle's emphasis was not on general laws in terms of which all things behaved. For him, each level of existence had laws of its own; a higher order, such as that of intelligent beings, cannot be explained by the same laws that govern inorganic matter. Each grade or class follows the law of its own nature and strives, in so far as it can, to realize its indwelling purpose. Man, since he is a self-conscious being, is at the top, and has a special "moral" responsibility. Each man has his own proper place or "station" in accordance with his degree of such responsibility. This is determined by his ability, through reason or faith, to understand the nature of the world and of his role therein.

Although, in the eyes of the Church, all souls were equal before God, all men were by no means equal here on earth. In fact, it is plain that the idea of the world as a "graded hierarchy" sanctioned, indeed made necessary, a political and social order that was not "democratic." It was, instead, frankly aristocratic, in that it taught that some men were fit to rule, others only to obey. We should remember that Aristotle himself had not challenged the existence of slavery in the society of his time. It had appeared to him an acceptable institution. We shall see later how the philosophic concepts underlying our nation made slavery unacceptable to us. But, for Aristotle, it had represented the lowest grade in the order of human society.

The importance of all this for our inquiry is that the medieval world picture was largely derived from philosophic concepts which supported and nourished a view of society that was not democratic. It lent itself to the acceptance of fixed social barriers, of the grading of privilege in accordance with inherited rank, of the right of some to decide for others. In fact, it provided a basis for the doctrine of the Divine Right of Kings. When we come to this realization we can see the need for recalling the medieval world picture as the background of the American Revolution.

But, whatever the excesses of the medieval view may have been, however much it held society in static molds, we must remember that this system, rooted in Aristotle, and shaped by Aquinas, was no thing of myth and superstition only. It had a satisfactory scientific and philosophical basis in the physics— and metaphysics—of Aristotle. It gave to men what seemed a sure ground for faith in God, and in a heaven where each would be rewarded in accordance with the degree to which he had realized, in his life on earth, the measure of purposefulness within him. It gave to men, too, a rational basis for the conviction that the universe had a purpose working all through it, and that man was God's warden here on earth. Most important, it provided a concept of the nature of man that gave significance to the life of each individual, for each should be permitted to develop himself as best he could, and each had a part to play in the great cosmic drama that had Earth, Heaven, and Hell as its three-level stage.

Man has never had a better ground for a sense of importance in the world, and of his responsibility for the fulfillment of a purpose inherent in all things. Despite all he has gained in terms of scientific knowledge and technical control of his environment, something was lost when the medieval picture of the world faded; something that had given man an almost irreplaceable sense of security within himself.

Soon we shall examine the reason why the medieval world picture, with its attendant dream of heaven, gave way to another picture, and another dream. The harps and trumpets of the angels grew faint, the cries of the damned were no longer heard clearly, the music of the spheres became inharmonious. But the panorama of the medieval concept of the world remains as the background for the modern mind. In fact, its forms and fears still throng the murky corridors of our subconsciousness.

3

Exit Aristotle—
Enter Newton

WHY DID the medieval world view wither? Why did men seek and find another view, and another dream? That must now be the direction of this inquiry.

Although the medieval world view gave a sense of basic purpose and meaning to the world, and although it gave an importance to the life of all men, it did sanction the grading of society into a sort of static hierarchy, and underwrote the unquestioning acceptance of authority. Furthermore, it gave no reason to hope for much improvement in the conditions of life here on earth. The compensating vision it offered was not of an ideal life here but only in heaven. Perhaps it could not have been otherwise. After the disintegration of the Roman world there were few indeed in Europe who had a tolerable existence. European man dwelt then—as he has often during later periods—

14

with slaughter and famine of his immediate neighbors. For millions of weary and frustrated souls there was only the hope of heaven, and the fear of hell, to give meaning to an otherwise miserable life. So faith sustained the suffering, illiterate masses. The educated few, those who could comprehend Aristotle and Aquinas, saw that only in heaven could the purpose that was in all things be fully revealed, only there could "form" completely triumph over matter.

So long as the scientific picture of the world on which this whole philosophic superstructure was reared persisted, faith and reason both supported the medieval view. We should remember that this scientific picture portrayed a flat earth at the center of the universe with heaven above—outside the spheres of the sun, moon, and stars—and hell below. This was the picture given poetic expression by Dante in his *Divine Comedy*. Moreover, each substance behaved and developed according to the particular laws of its own nature. Later we shall see how these major premises of the whole Aristotelian view broke down. But there were other reasons, too, for the collapse of the medieval picture.

Most important among these was a radical change in the attitude of men towards established authority. This increased, of course, proportionately with the increasing conviction that such authority rested upon scientific and philosophic foundations that were no longer secure. But we can illustrate the change in question best by a quotation, from Pope Leo XIII. Pope Leo, writing in a later time, said, "That fatal and deplorable passion for innovation which was aroused in the sixteenth century first threw the Christian world into confusion, and then, by natural sequence, passed on to philosophy and thence pervaded all ranks of society. From this source issued those maxims of unbridled liberty—the chief one of which proclaims that all men are by race and nature alike—that each is so far master of himself as in no way to come under the authority of another; that he is free to think on any subject as he likes.

. . . In a society founded upon these principles government is only the will of the people. . . ."

Pope Leo still held the Aristotelian world view. His sense of outrage against another attitude is obvious. But the amazing thing about his statement is that the principles which he so furiously denounces are the very ones in which we passionately believe, upon which our nation is founded, and which we will die to defend. What brought about this complete reversal of values by which the anathema of one age became the credo of another? Here, in this one passage, is the essence of the change from the medieval to the modern attitude. The former held that there should be an orderly, graded society in which each man had his proper station, and in which those in the lower ranks must accept the authority of those above them. The latter holds that society is made up of free and equal men each one of whom has the right to his own opinion on any matter.

But Pope Leo was certainly wrong in attributing the origins of this change to a "fatal and deplorable passion for innovation." It was nothing so capricious. It began, rather, because men of science were beginning a period of experimentation and observation which led them to believe that the scientific premises of the Aristotelian world picture were no longer satisfactory.

The new revolution in thought, the birth of a new concept of the world and a new attendant dream, was one that took a long time to become effective—and to "pervade all ranks of society." In fact, the dates of its beginning and of its completion are hard to define. Your scientist may tell you it began with Copernicus, at the end of the fifteenth century. Your philosopher may hold that it did not really get under way until the time of René Descartes, more than one hundred years later. Your literary friend may insist that its tone and character were set by Montaigne, who lived about halfway between.

In any case, the new revolution was marked by certain unmistakable characteristics. In science there was a new insistence upon careful experimentation under controlled conditions. Neither the Scholastics, nor, indeed, their revered Aristotle, had made much use of these methods. In philosophy the new trend was marked by a determination to take nothing for granted on the basis of "authority," and to accept only the fewest and simplest theories necessary to interpret the current observations of science. Gone was the medieval docility in accepting authority, and the medieval delight in complicated and involved explanations. In literature three new trends should be noted: an interest in this world rather than in heaven and hell; a passionate insistence on the right to deal with all subjects; and a marked skepticism with regard to established authority. Common to all was that hallmark of the Renaissance—man's determination to think for himself.

For our own convenience, we shall consider the period with which we are dealing as beginning with the birth of Copernicus in 1473, and as ending with the death of John Locke in 1704. Copernicus began the ground swell of new theories which unsettled the foundation of the Aristotelian world picture. Locke derived, from the new picture which resulted, the political and social doctrines on which our nation still rests.

Copernicus, in his early studies in his native Poland, and elsewhere, had noted that certain motions of the moon and major planets could not easily be explained on the basis of the theory that the earth was the center of the universe. Infected with the new spirit of free inquiry, he was troubled. To explain the observable motions of the heavenly bodies in terms of the orthodox, "Ptolemaic" hypothesis required many fanciful elaborations according to which the stars behaved like stunt flyers. But on the basis of the daring and heretical sun-center hypothesis their motions could be simply and convincingly explained. The Church had condemned this theory, and, in the face of its fierce opposition, there was little that Copernicus could do to spread his discoveries among more than a learned and radical few. But a relentless doubt was born regarding the correctness of the "official" concept. This doubt would not let the inquiring spirit of man rest until he had shattered one world picture and constructed another.

One hundred years later, we can imagine Galileo, armed with a telescope, which Copernicus had lacked, climbing the Leaning Tower in Pisa. Watching the stars through the soft Italian nights, he substantiated the observation and reaffirmed the theories of his predecessor. From the same tower we know he dropped objects of various kinds, while his students in the square below calculated their rate of descent. Galileo found that, allowing only for differing air resistance, all the objects fell with the same velocity. He realized, therefore, that all objects obey one fundamental law, that of gravitation, irrespective of their nature. He began to wonder if there might not be a number of such natural laws, the operation of which determined the behavior of all things—inanimate, living, and human. Such speculations were absolutely opposed by the Aristotelian view that each sort of substance obeyed laws of its own inner nature, laws determined by the special "form" indwelling in each.

Not until another hundred years had passed did Isaac Newton, the great English mathematician and physicist, develop a completed world view that entirely unsettled the foundations of the older, traditional picture. Whether or not the apple of legend bounced from his head, Newton became deeply concerned with a single fundamental law of gravitation, and with other such universal laws which were to be accepted as the foundation for all the science of the modern world until the new developments of our own century.

Before going on to describe the new concepts of the world, of matter, and of man, that came with Newton, we should pause to consider other changes that were going on as the middle ages gave way to modern times.

A fresh wind of restlessness was blowing across the western

world. Its effects took many turns. But, by and large, these all had to do with man's new preoccupation with this earth itself, with its breadth and its beauty, and with the possibilities for a better life upon it. There were many reasons for this shift in the center of man's interests from the heaven he believed was above him to the earth he knew was around him.

In the first place, there had been, beginning in the early fifteenth century, or before, the rediscovery of the art of antiquity with its keen, honest love of earthly beauty. The effect of this rapidly permeated the art of the Renaissance. Then there had been the invention of the compass, which had enabled bold men to set out on voyages of discovery, and soon to prove, by the incontrovertible feat of circumnavigation, that the earth was indeed round, and to find it full of rich new lands. The effect this had on men's imaginations can never be repeated—unless one day we can voyage among the stars.

All these things influenced European man profoundly. The beauty of flesh and of landscape blossomed in painting. The ships of Europe slanted through the seas of all the world. Men set forth to seek a better life in the new lands, and began to demand that better life here on earth instead of in heaven. Old visions of Utopian lands, ancient as history, were re-activated, and men dreamed of their actual establishment.

Along with these developments, it was inevitable that there should be an impatience with established authority, and a questioning of all accepted premises. Men wished to explore the unknown reaches of their minds as they had the uncharted seas of their earth. Science chafed at the restraints placed upon it by the Church which, as late as 1633, when the English settlements in Massachusetts and Virginia were already thriving, condemned Galileo for accepting the "Copernican Hypothesis," and forced him to recant. René Descartes, though himself a loyal Catholic, decided that, in seeking Truth, nothing was to be taken as true—not God, not the soul—until Reason proved it true.

But it was Isaac Newton who picked up the pieces of the puzzle of the world, and fitted them into a new design, which has remained the basis of scientific and philosophic interpretation of the world until our own time. Newton's friend, John Locke, derived from the new world picture a new theory of the nature of man, and of religious and political society, which is still the basis of our nation, and which still permeates our minds and hearts, our attitudes and prejudices. With Newton and Locke, therefore, the whole tremendous revolution in man's thinking which marked the transition to modern times found its culmination and completion.

The world picture which Newton developed was the result of some of the most brilliant and original thinking in history. It gave a form that seemed final and acceptable to the long process of the liberation of science from subjection to the Aristotelian premises of the medieval Church. Yet it is interesting to note that Newton, despite his reduction of the behavior of the universe to a few simple, mechanical laws, remained a devout Christian, and was still very much under the medieval influence.

Newton's work in physics and mathematics represented exactly the same spirit of free inquiry, and individual responsibility for its results, which had characterized the work of the great leaders of the Protestant Reformation in the field of religious thought. Luther, Calvin, Huss, and their fellows had insisted on seeking God and Eternal Truth each in his own way. Each had felt the rapture of direct communication which is the greatest reward that the independent spirit of Protestantism could find. Each denied, at least for himself, the necessity of one established church as intermediary between God and man. This daring feat of mind was a vital factor in the preparation for a new world picture which was to have its exact, scientific portrayal in the writings of Newton.

What was this new picture? How did it portray the pattern of our universe and describe the laws according to which it functioned?

In the Newtonian picture, the earth is no longer the center of the universe; it is a minor planet, subject to exactly the same laws as are all others. With Newton this was so clearly established that the Church soon thereafter had to drop its opposition to the hated hypothesis of Copernicus. Gravitation and a few other basic laws explain the behavior of the universe. Moreover, all objects on the earth and in the skies obey these few, immutable laws irrespective of their own particular nature. And indwelling Purpose was not set forth as one of those laws. Soon, Newton's follower, the Frenchman Laplace, was to say, when asked if he believed in God, "I see no need for such an hypothesis."

To explain the pull of gravitation upon every part of every object, Newton was driven to the theory that all objects of all kinds were made up of uniform, microscopic atoms. These atoms are always alike; it is their different configurations that characterize different kinds of objects. Basically, the atoms of a man's body are the same as those of his dog, his house, or the very earth he plows.

This was not the first time that such an "atomic" theory had appeared; it had been well known to the Greeks. But, as in the case of the sun-center theory of the universe, also known to them, Aristotle had rejected it. It is easy to see how poorly either of these theories would have been suited to the medieval world view, which needed to have the earth the center of all, and to suppose an essential difference in the nature of different substances.

There is another very important implication of the atomic theory as to the nature of all matter. For, in themselves, the atoms which make up all things in the world have none of the qualities which seem to us to characterize each thing, and by means of which, indeed, we identify and distinguish them. Galileo had begun to point this out; with Newton it became fully established. Although at first it may seem to be unimportant, it was the origin of a whole new definition of the nature of man. We must consider it in detail.

For Aristotle, the rose was red because *redness* was an intrinsic quality of its own nature. The fire was hot because heat was a part of its elemental character. But it now became clear that this is not so. Colors, sounds, odors, heat and cold, are not qualities which "inhere" in the things we see and hear and taste. They are qualities which appear to *us* to do so because they are immediately engendered by our contacts with things outside us. But how is this possible? And what implication does it have with regard to our own nature, to the nature, that is, of *man?*

The answer which John Locke gave to this question will take us to a new definition of the nature of the human being—one on which the political and social bases of the United States still rest.

We must remember that this question as to the nature of man was not an arbitrary or capricious one. When man completely redefines the nature of his world he is forced to redefine himself. In our own day the world awaits such another redefinition.

So long as man accepted the world picture of Aristotle, that of a purposeful, properly ordered universe, the position and nature of the human being was clear. Man was the chief actor in a drama planned by God, with the earth, the center of the universe, as his stage. In everything an innate purposefulness was gradually revealing itself; man, the being in which the ascending order of creatures culminated, was himself aware of that purposefulness, knew himself as a part of the cosmic drama being played, and was in part responsible for its success or its failure. He was an immediate and necessary part of that drama. His life was purposeful, and was endowed accordingly with a clear meaning. No wonder that the world picture of Aristotle, as shaped by Aquinas, could give a rich sense of satisfaction to those who sufficiently understood it.

But once you accept the Newtonian picture, what becomes of the position of man therein? You find yourself in a mechanically moving universe made up of uniform atoms forming and reforming into different material substances, of which man is one. Or is he perhaps in some way different? Here is where the problem of qualities such as colors, sounds, and odors becomes of unsuspected importance.

It is all very well to conceive, as the Newtonian view requires us to do, that the universe is really made up of colorless, soundless, odorless atoms forming and reforming into a myriad different substances, in accordance with a few fixed and unchangeable laws, in infinite space and infinite time. But that isn't the way it looks and sounds and smells to us. Newton himself realized that a distinction must be drawn between the world as it was for science, and the world as it was for the ordinary observer. The first was a world of absolute, true space and time, in which the material atoms whirled on and on in accordance with the laws that governed their behavior. The second was the world as we know it through our senses, one of relative, apparent space and time. In this world, the individual finds his way about by the usual signposts of colors, sounds, tastes, sensations of all kinds.

Newton also made a distinction between "primary qualities" (those which he thought were really *in* things—like extension, the quality of "taking up space") and "secondary qualities" (the very colors, sounds, etc., of which we have been speaking). It is these secondary qualities, and the manner in which they are engendered, that give a clue as to the true nature of the human being.

In the Newtonian world picture, man had knowledge both of the world as experienced through his senses, and as conceived by his reason. In his direct experience, man was constantly aware of many "qualities," the very existence of which, independent of his experience, could not be established. Yet man, in observing the universe, was really aware of it only in terms of these "secondary qualities." How was this possible? What was the peculiar nature of the human being which made it so?

This was the inescapable question which John Locke had in

mind when he set himself the task of defining the nature of man in accordance with the concepts shaped by his good friend, Isaac Newton. Locke had been born near Bristol, England, in 1632. He had studied at Oxford, and later became secretary to Lord Shaftesbury and was involved in the changing political fortunes of the latter. At one time Locke was exiled to Holland by the government of Charles II. He returned with William of Orange at the time of his accession to the English throne in 1689. Thereafter, Locke settled down to a career of writing, and became an authority on philosophy and its application to political and religious theory.

As he faced the problem of the nature of man, Locke may well have said to himself, "What is the nature of the human being who is both the observer of the world as it appears to his senses, and also the interpreter of the world as Newton has shown it to be?" He saw that the human being was the only meeting point between the "two worlds," and that their meeting was characterized by the appearance, in the very act of sense experience, of the "secondary qualities" of color, sound, scent, heat, cold, etc. It seemed clear that the clue as to the special nature of man lay in this phenomenon, which occurred in his observation of the world.

One answer to the question of the nature of the human being had already been given by Thomas Hobbes. He had held that the human "observer" was, like everything else in Newton's merry-go-round, a particular sort of "material substance," one particular pattern of the omnipresent atoms. But, for Locke, this was not satisfactory. Those material atoms were the stuff out of which all else, including man's *body,* was made, true. But they were not the stuff from which man's *mind* was made. For, if man were nothing more than just another "material substance," if he were not different, if, in him, something new had not been added, how could the appearance of "secondary qualities" ever be explained? And the fact that they *did* appear, in the interaction between what was outside of man and what was within him, was proof that there was something about the human being that made him different.

Locke, therefore, was driven to the conclusion that the human being must be, or must contain, a special sort of substance which he named a "mental substance." The essential character of this type of substance was, said Locke, that it was just so constituted that—when it was acted upon by all kinds of material substances—it was aware of them, not as they really were in their own nature, but in terms of those very "secondary qualities" out of which all our direct experience of the world is compounded. Man, so far as his physical body is concerned, is a material substance like everything else in the universe, and subject to all the same laws. But man, in addition, is also a mental substance. As such he has the unique ability to sense the world in terms of "secondary qualities" and yet to interpret it as he conceives it to be in its own nature. This unique ability constitutes his nature and function; it distinguishes him from everything else on earth. Its possession gives him his claim to a special importance; its exercise is his special responsibility.

The medieval world view had necessitated a concept of the human being which gave to man a sense of belonging to, and participating in, a drama of development directed by God. He felt himself a part of that larger whole, and knew he must accept his own proper role therein, be it great or small.

But the Newtonian world view produced, with Locke, a concept of the human being which gave to a man a sense of the importance of using his own individual *reason* to interpret the world in accordance with the experience of it which his senses brought to him. That, in doing so, men would become aware of the existence of God, and of the truths of religious teaching, Newton and Locke never doubted. But in their interpretation of the world, and of man, there is no logical *need* for men to do so, or to control their behavior accordingly.

We are now done with the philosophic background for John

Locke's definition of the human individual as a "mental sub-stance." We are ready to turn to the implications for religious, political, and social theories which that definition carried within it. These were the very implications which were the chief influences that shaped the American "Way of Life."

4

John Locke—Man as the Power of Reason

IN HIS *Origins of the American Revolution,* John C. Miller says ". . . it is not too much to say that during the era of the American Revolution the 'party line' was John Locke. . . ." The Declaration of Independence and the Constitution itself were as much an embodiment of Locke's principles as was the formation of Soviet Russia an embodiment of the principles of Karl Marx.

First, it will be well to point out that while Locke was the chief determining influence in the formulation of the basic principles of our nation, he was by no means the only one.

The first settlers of this country, predominantly English as they were, came to New England and Virginia before Locke was born. It was in the century and a half that intervened between their arrival and the Revolution that Newton redefined man. But the very nature of the new country, and the exploits of those who explored and settled it were themselves factors favorable to the development of Locke's ideas. There could have been no more fertile soil for the roots which his ideas provided for the growth of "Rugged Individualism."

The wide new world, with its seemingly limitless space and opportunity, would itself have made the early citizens of the American colonies a freedom-loving people. Especially was this true because those who crossed the "western ocean" were, for the most part, already in search of freedom, religious or political. But, in the growth of our country, from the original colonies, through the Revolution, and into the United States, we find a marvelous instance of the favorable interaction of an underlying phliosophy with just the sort of locale and condition of life best suited for its development.

Of course very few early Americans had read Locke. But many of the most influential among them had done so. Thomas Jefferson was steeped in his philosophy and political theory. Locke's theories, by way of the thinking and writing of Jefferson and of other great early figures in our history, gradually permeated the whole American scene. Before going on to demonstrate this, we must develop further the implications of Locke's definition of the human individual.

Each human individual, according to Locke, is a "mental substance." We should note the use of that word "substance." In the Newtonian world view it was a criterion of reality. Anything which could be accepted as real had to be thought of as a substance. This was the natural result of a view which held that all things were made up of material atoms. Furthermore, this identification of reality with "substance" has persisted into our own days and still dominates the thinking of the majority of us. We are still children of the Newtonian view, and only a few of us fully realize that for contemporary physics substance has lost almost all substantiality. The basic reality seems to be a sort of all pervasive energy. The fact that matter can explode into energy has been all too well established by the terrible demonstration of the atom bomb.

When each individual is born, said Locke, the nature of his "mental substance" is that of a "blank tablet." Experience, in the form of contacts with material and other mental substances, writes upon this tablet the record that constitutes his life. At birth there are absolutely no "innate ideas," nor are there any innate moral principles. Absolutely all of our knowledge, and of our moral codes as well, comes from sensation. It comes directly in the form of "simple ideas," or, through the activity of reason in comparing and arranging these, indirectly, as general concepts, rules, and principles of conduct. Even the idea of God itself comes only to each individual through his own experience.

Such a concept of the nature of the human individual had at once revolutionary implications. It gave a philosophic ground for the theory that all men are created equal and free. If mental substances are "blank tablets" at birth, there is no reason whatsoever for one man to claim any natural superiority over another. All reason for doing so depends upon the inheritance of some special prerogatives. Therefore, man was given, by Locke's theory of his nature, a deeper and sounder reason for insistence on the equality of all men than he had ever had before.

Furthermore, all men were born to be free as well as equal. This followed because, in the absence of any inherited superiority, no man had any natural authority over other men—neither in church nor in state. Any authority worthy of the respect of free and equal "mental substances" was merely the result of their common, voluntary agreement, and merely served their convenience.

These are the most important general implications of Locke's theory as to the nature of the human individual. Now we shall see how they were developed more in detail, first in the field of religion, then, at greater length, in the field of politics.

Until the eighteenth century, Protestantism had not really

been "tolerant." That is, the major Protestant sects, those stemming from Luther, Calvin, as well as the Church of England, had required rigid adherence to dogmas and, in some cases, rituals, of their own. While the sole authority of Rome had been overthrown, the idea of church authority in general, the idea that an ordinary mortal, at least, should put his soul in the care of a church, and his faith in the principles of a sect, was not generally questioned. True "Freedom of Religion" had by no means been established. We need only recall the furious intolerance of the Puritans of Massachusetts Bay, and the flight of the liberal Roger Williams to Rhode Island, to give a case in point.

With the growing influence of Locke's theories, there emerged a perfect philosophic basis for complete religious tolerance, for that very insistence upon freedom of worship which has become one of the bulwarks of our beliefs. Let us see why this was so.

Not only were Locke's mental substances born free and equal; he never developed any clear explanation for any system by which one was related to another. Whatever relations actually developed among them certainly did not give any of them any authority over any others except by mutual agreement. In Locke's view there was no reason for any ascending order, any natural hierarchy of persons, as there had been in the medieval view based on Aristotle. This held true in the field of religion as well as in that of politics.

Locke makes this very clear. He says, "The care of every man's soul belongs to himself, and is to be left to himself." A man who wishes to save his soul knows best how to do so, for he himself is most concerned in the endeavor. He does not need the guidance of anyone else "who may be as ignorant of the way as myself, and who certainly is less concerned for my salvation than I myself am. . . ."

On the basis of Locke's premises, religion becomes a matter of introspection only; there is no necessary reference to established authority. Why not, if each man must discover the ideas of God, right, wrong, and immortality for himself? If this be so, each individual is the best judge of the correctness of his own religion, and one man cannot be shown to be incorrect in his belief—which may be wrong for others but right for *him*. Let us remember again that this was a revolutionary attitude not only in the opinion of the Catholic world, but also in that of the early Protestant sects as well. Yet it took root so early in our history that we hardly remember the bitter religious intolerance of our earliest Colonial communities, and are ashamed when we are reminded of it. Ralph Waldo Emerson, in saying, "The wise man needs no Church, for he is the prophet" was giving expression to the ultimate development of Locke's point of view toward religion.

Locke not only believed that "the care of every man's soul belongs to himself," but also that no man was under any obligation to join any church, nor was any man born into membership in one. In discussing the organization of a church, Locke wrote, "I say it is a free and voluntary society. Nobody is born a member of any church—since the joining together of several members into this church society is absolutely free and spontaneous, it necessarily follows that the right of making its laws can belong to none but the society itself." Thus no church, except by the voluntary agreement of its members, need have any connection with other such groups, or with any higher or central authorities. Again, one can see how violently opposed such a view was to that which had prevailed in medieval times. One can equally well see that here, in Locke's theory as to the nature of man, is the foundation in philosophy for our traditional attitude toward religion, at least among the Protestant churches. Freedom of religion is a slogan which we will still defend; sometimes we forget, however, that our traditions also support the freedom *not* to believe.

Now we are ready to plunge into what will constitute the heart of the first section of this whole inquiry—the effect of

Locke's ideas on the political framework and functioning of the government of the United States.

One very good thing about John Locke was that he wrote fine, clear prose, prose which could be understood by any intelligent man. Perhaps young Thomas Jefferson may not have been familiar with all of Locke's monumental *Essay Concerning Human Understanding.* But he certainly knew intimately the far more compact, and far more effective, treatise called *An Essay Concerning the True Original Extent and End of Civil Government.* The impact of this historic essay, its permeating and lasting influence, was due, no doubt, as much to its simple and familiar language as to its philosophic depth.

Locke begins his essay on Civil Government by saying that, in order to understand the nature of political power, "we must consider what state all men are naturally in, and that is a state of perfect freedom to order their actions and dispose of their possessions and persons as they think fit." This original condition of man is "A state also of equality, wherein all the power and jurisdiction is reciprocal, no one having more than another."

In other words, Locke's "mental substances," before they begin in any way to organize, by their common consent, any system of government, are perfectly free and perfectly equal in what Locke calls the "state of nature."

Now this seems to us rather hard to swallow. Since Locke's time we have learned enough about primitive societies to know that ignorance, superstition, and tabu keep their members far from perfect freedom, and inherited prerogatives far from perfect equality. But we must remember that in Locke's day several strong influences had combined to give a romanticized view of the savage life. There was the deep anger at the frivolity and corruption of existing autocratic governments. There was the recent discovery of many well-organized civil communities far from Europe—in Asia, and in Central and South America. There was the myth of the "noble savage," a being superior to the demoralized denizens of effete societies. Soon Jean Jacques Rousseau was to denounce all governments and call for a return to the "state of nature." Thus we can, perhaps, see why Locke held so apparently naive a view.

Furthermore, Locke believed that men in a state of nature were subject to a "law of nature," a law which disposes men, out of insistence on their own "natural rights," to respect those of others. Here, too, Locke's view seems almost smugly ingenuous. But we must remember that he lived in a time when men, rebelling against all established authority, and demanding the right to think for themselves, still held that man was naturally rational, and that, therefore, *reason* would guide him even in his original state. In our day, we are less certain of this. In our troubled times man has given far more rein to his passions than to his reason. But his coming deeds cast no shadows before on Locke's Age of Enlightenment.

If men in a state of nature enjoyed such perfect freedom and equality, and if the law of nature protected them from any excessive disorder, why did they ever choose to subject themselves to any system of civil governments? Why did they not, instead, remain in that happy aboriginal state? In the terms of Locke's own language, why should any group of "mental substances" limit their natural freedom, and threaten their natural equality, by organizing any such system?

Right away Locke connects his answer to this inevitable question with the desire of men better to protect their *property*. We should point out at once that by property Locke usually meant man's "life, liberty, and estate." That is, his concept of "property" includes man's bodily security, man's physical and mental freedom, *as well as man's belongings*. We should always keep this in mind because this concept of "property" is basic in all Locke's political theories.

Men, in the state of nature, "for the most part contented themselves with what unassisted nature offered to their necessities." In other words, in that mythical summertime the living was easy enough to content them without undue effort. But men then began to improve the primitive weapons with which they hunted, the crude tools with which they tilled the soil, and the character of their rough dwellings. He who, by his own *labor,* improved the weapon or the tool or the dwelling, had the right to call his *own* that which he had improved.

Locke used the example of the improvement of a bit of land by the labor of a particular individual, and said of this, "It being by him removed from the common state nature placed it in, it hath by this labor something annexed to it that excludes the right of other men." Look closely at this argument. Here we have the very genesis, the philosophic root, of our traditional attitude towards "private property." What a man has labored to improve is to be recognized by other men as his own. It is easy to understand how this basic idea, while by no means peculiar to the American scene, has flourished here with particular vigor. For no other setting could so have favored its development as that of a vast new land in which he who improves the earth and uncovers its resources feels unquestionably entitled to call his own that which he has improved.

It is interesting and important to note here that Locke placed some limitations upon the right of any individual to appropriate land and resources. Very little attention has been paid to these limitations, and in our more crowded and exploited earth they deserve wide notice. We shall return to them later.

Basically, it is their desire to protect their property, their persons *and* possessions, that impels men to set up civil governments, and thus to limit their "natural" freedom and equality. Locke traces very clearly how this comes about. In the state of nature, each man is the sole protector of his own property—of his life, liberty, and estate. If his property is in any way threatened, there is no one pledged to help him guard it. Now, if all men were equally industrious by nature, this would not matter. But unfortunately, this is not true. Some men will labor and thus create additional property for themselves. But others, less constrained by the "law of nature," will be tempted to take what is not theirs by right of labor, and some will succumb to that temptation. For, although all mental substances are born equal, they do not all develop into beings equally wise, or equally moral. None have any "inherent" ideas or moral principles, and experience gives differing degrees of wisdom, and differing standards of conduct.

Moreover, it is not always convenient, or practical, for each individual to be the constant guardian of all that is his own. Nor is it easy for each individual to have to devise himself the punishment due anyone who attacks his property. For their own convenience, therefore, men become disposed to set up a society which has "itself the power to preserve the property and . . . punish the offenses of all those" who are its members.

Notice that Locke's definition of property, as broad enough to include life, liberty, *and* estate, makes it logical to conceive of the need for government as arising from a desire for better safeguarding of liberties *and* protection of "estate." It shows why Locke felt that protection of property in the narrower sense of "belongings" was as important a function of government as the safeguarding of life and liberty. Government accomplishes both these functions by providing improved means of protection, and agreed-upon rules for the punishment of offenders.

This is made possible because each individual gives up his own "natural" right of protecting his property, and of punishing offenders against it, to the community. Locke says, "there, and there only, is political society, where every one of its members hath quitted this natural power, resigned it up into the hands of the community." Thus men who enter into such a society shift from themselves as individuals to the community as their agent the power to protect their persons and possessions and to punish those who threaten or attack those of others. Thus the community, "by understanding indifferent laws [Locke means, by agreeing upon just laws] and by men authorized by the community for their execution, decides all the differences that may happen between any members of that society."

It is the individual members of such a community who grant to it the powers it possesses. There is never any doubt about that. No other righteous source of political power exists. A true political society of this kind can be set up only by the consent of every individual who is to be a member of it. For the very essence of such a community is that everyone within it must be equally subject to its laws, and equally obligated to obey those who are chosen to enforce them. Thus Locke says that in an absolute monarchy no true political community exists because there are those who stand outside the law, notably the King himself.

This same defect, we may well note, is particularly true in the case of the modern totalitarian state.

What have we found out so far about the influence of Locke's essay on the formation of our nation? Already we can see, emerging from it, the bases of those great political principles which undergird and sustain the "community" which has become the United States. For Locke held that all men are by nature free and equal, and gave a philosophic ground for this that was complete and sure. He held that a true political system can be formed, and a true community be said to exist, only when such free and equal men willingly transfer to it their natural rights to protect their lives, liberties, and estates. And he held, also, that the chief function of government, its very reason for existence, is to protect the "property" of its citizens.

Despite all the incredible changes in our world, despite all that men have suffered and dreamed since Locke's time, despite other new theories of The State, the principles Locke laid down are still a fundamental part of the American scene.

Government by will of the people! To us, with our political heritage, it seems obvious that any other basis for the authority of government is outrageously wrong. To deny that the will of the people is the only just ground for a system of government seems to us as wrong as to argue against the rightness of the multiplication tables. It appears to us to have almost the same objective reality. Yet remember how Pope Leo railed against this very principle.

How does the will of the people express itself? How, on the basis of its guidance, are those decisions made which are necessary for the functioning of government? We do not lack quick answers to these questions. The opinion of the majority provides us with a sure guide. We can find a definitive statement endorsing this principle of majority decision in Locke's Essay. He says that when any number of men have made a community "by the consent of every individual," they thereby endow that community "with power to act as one body." Such action must be "only by the will and determination of the majority." Naturally, because that which motivates "any community being only the consent of the individuals of it, and it being one body must move one way, it is necessary the body should move that way whither the greater force carries it, which is the consent of the majority."

Now, in a very profound and unmistakable manner, this doctrine, so traditional, indeed so necessary, to the western, democratic world, substitutes the will of the people, as expressed through majority decision, for the will of God, as interpreted by the Church. That is why Pope Leo feared it so. Not only was it incompatible with dogmatic religion but in theory it might lead to a decision to undertake the conquest of the world by the most invidious and shameless use of brutal power. There could be a decision that one race is superior to all others, and has, therefore, the right to such a course of conquest. Or the majority could decide that only one political creed was right, and that all other creeds, all dissenting opinions, must be ruthlessly suppressed.

In theory all this could happen. But in fact when such decisions have been made, they have not come as the result of the expression of the free will of a free electorate. The evidence is strongly to the contrary for history itself records the fact that the really vicious choices of policy—such as those mentioned above—have been made by despotic rulers, or by the control of a "one-party" political system.

Majority decisions made in the United States with regard, for example, to foreign policy, have often been damaging to the world, and thus to ourselves. Excessive tariffs, lack of world responsibility in measure with our power, attempts at "neutrality," at war evasion rather than war prevention, all these have caused distress and insecurity, and have opened the way to war. But the decisions underlying them have been brought about by stupidity and lack of foresight, not by any real and demonstrable viciousness.

For such a society as Locke describes, in which the members give up to the community the protection of their property, and in which community action depends upon majority decision, certain prerequisites are needed. First, a large number of the members of the community must have some property beyond their lives and liberties, some "estate" to protect. Second, enough of them must have sufficient education to ensure that majority decisions will, on the whole, be wise.

Locke himself points up the first of these prerequisites. He says, of his political doctrine, "It necessarily supposes and requires that the people should have property," and here he must have been referring to "possessions." No such supposition could have been made, no such requirement met, in Russia in 1917. But there, as we shall see, the revolution which established the Soviet Union was inspired by totally different doctrines.

In the case of the United States, in the days of our revolution, could the requirement "that the people should have property" be met? Certainly there were many thousands who had none. The poor starving soldiers who fought partly for liberty, and partly for food, often had no possessions of their own. But those who were directly responsible for the formulation of our country did have property in this sense—whether it was a large plantation or a log hut. Together with them stood the land owners, large and small, the country squire, the shop keeper, and the hill farmer. In that day of unlimited promise, those who lacked land and homes were sure they could secure both in the vast new world around them.

Thomas Jefferson, whose fertile mind was impregnated by Locke's theories, saw the need for trying to continue a sufficient distribution of property if a truly democratic nation were to develop. He realized the dangers inherent in having too much wealth concentrated in the hands of too few. Thus he tried to block such a development among the landed gentry of his native Virginia by recommending an abolishment of the law of "primogeniture," by which the eldest son inherited the whole estate of his father. Jefferson also, as Northrop says, "was fearful of the effect upon democracy of the development of an industrial society in the United States." He feared it "because of the concentration of private property in the hands of a few which it might produce, and the evils of congested city life which it creates."

Within Jefferson's time, these alarming results of the Industrial Revolution were already well under way in England, and he foresaw that they would soon develop in his own beloved country. Perhaps he even foresaw, in a general way, that those very evils—too much for the few, too little for the many—of unbridled industrial development in its early days would be a stimulus to a revolt against a "free" democratic society. But he could not have foreseen the strange turn which Karl Marx was to give to such a revolt.

Locke also assumes the existence of some education among those who set up a political society. For he says, "The freedom of man . . . is grounded on his having reason. To turn him loose to an unrestrained liberty before he has reason to guide him is . . . to thrust him out amongst brutes, and abandon him to a state as wretched . . . as theirs." Thus Locke finds it to be the duty of parents to see to it that children are restrained until their reason develops. Jefferson, always Locke's disciple, saw that the state must take up the burden of education. He wrote, "Establish the law for educating the common people. This it is the business of the state to effect, and on a general plan." Universal education is always the cornerstone of any democracy. But it can be used to stimulate freedom of thought, or to indoctrinate those educated with one set of political, social, or religious theories and to close their minds to all others.

We have seen that rising nationalism ending in the sudden independence of peoples lacking even an educated minority can cause or rather result in chaos; the case of the Congo typifies the potentiality. This bears out Locke's view.

We are guilty of one serious failure in our approach to education in the United States. We shall do well to remember that, if education is to retain a vital sense of significance, it indeed "must concern itself not merely with applied science, and literature, and art, and practical matters, but also with man's basic beliefs concerning the nature of himself and his universe." This, most of us would agree, the ordinary process of education in this country does not sufficiently do. When we think about this, we are aware of the lack of any general, philosophic, or moral concepts about man and his world that serve to remind us of the philosophic bases of our society.

It is this very lack that has recently rendered us unsure of the continuing firmness of those foundations that support our type of state and way of life. We can overcome such a lack only by examining those foundations in the light of the realities of our present world, and by satisfying ourselves about their solidity, with whatever additions such new conditions require.

5

The United States—
The State as the
Protector of Liberty

WE HAVE had enough now of the *general* influence of
Locke upon the development of our country. What
remains is to show the direct and detailed effect of his works
on the actual writing of the documents that marked its birth
and confirmation: the Declaration and the Constitution.

We had better turn to the last section of Locke's work,
which was called "Of the Ends of Political Society and Government." Here we shall find most clearly stated the essence of
Locke's whole political theory. Here, too, was the focal point
of the profound influence that theory had on the actual shaping
of the United States, in terms of the forms and functions of our
system of state, and on our basic attitudes and prejudices about
government.

In this final section of his essay on government, Locke repeats, in a sort of outline form, the reasons why men are willing to quit the freedom and equality of the state of nature, and to set up governments. Basically, as we have already seen, this is because, in the state of nature, man will find that "the enjoyment of the property he has in this state is very unsafe, very insecure." For, in the state of nature, many things are wanting for the adequate protection of property. Locke lists three chief "wants."

First, the want of "an established, settled, known law" acknowledged "by common consent to be the standard of right and wrong."

Second, the want of "a known and indifferent judge, with authority to determine all differences according to the established law."

Third, the want of any power to stand in back of such law and such judge, and to make effective the provisions of the law and the decisions of the judge.

These are the three chief "wants" of the state of nature that drive men to forsake it for an organized community. But Locke looks with a sort of nostalgic regret upon the fact that men must be so driven. He says, "And were it not for the corruption and viciousness of degenerate men there would be no need of any other [community than that of 'nature'], no necessity that men should separate from this great and natural community, and associate into lesser combinations." But since, alas, this cannot be, men, in associating into "lesser combinations," must carefully consider just what powers they give up to these communities, and in what degree.

We shall find that the powers man surrendered to the community are two. First, the power to do whatsoever seems best to protect his own life, liberty, and estate. This he gives up only in part, in so far as the best interests of the new community he is forming require. Second, he gives up, and in this case completely, the power to punish those who injure his "property." The individual gives these powers over to the community which is then "obliged to secure everyone's property by providing against those three defects [our three 'wants'] that made the state of nature so unsafe and uneasy."

Our Declaration of Independence embodies the general principles of Locke's political theories. Those great truths which the Declaration holds to be "self-evident," those fountainheads of American freedom, what are they but the embodiment in a national charter of John Locke's philosophic mainsprings? That all men are created free and equal, that they are endowed with unalienable rights, that it is to secure these rights that governments are set up—these are the first foundations of our national life.

It had required Locke's new definition of the nature of man to give a firm philosophic ground for the idea that men have "unalienable rights," for the idea that true government is by will of the people, and for the idea that the end of government is to protect the life, liberty, and "pursuit of happiness" of the governed. Note that this last phrase, which was Jefferson's, is a more inclusive and a more winning phrase than "accumluation of property." Nevertheless, that natural activity of the independent individual may well be considered a legitimate part of the pursuit of happiness.

We must make it very clear that Locke's concept of the human being was the necessary prerequisite for any such principles of politics. Locke's "mental substances," as he conceived them, were really free and independent in a deeper sense than man had ever before conceived himself to be. For "blank tablets" are all the same. If none of these had any "innate ideas" pre-inscribed on them, all men really did have the same start, the same rights, and should have the same opportunities. If only through their mutual consent did they abandon the state of nature for organized communities, then the sole authority of governments came from the consent of the governed. If men organized such communities for the better protection of their properties, then the original and proper function of government was to give the minimum necessary protection to the life, liberty, and estates of its inhabitants, and to punish offenders against its citizens. Any extension of these powers of government was to be resisted.

Furthermore, Locke had given a ground for the American Revolution in his insistence that an absolute monarchy was no true political society. We should note here that England never fully and vehemently waged war against the colonies for more than one reason. She was, of course, deeply involved in a series of wars with France. But also many of her politicians and her people were themselves steeped in the political principles of Locke. They lacked, therefore, a philosophic ground for pursuing the struggle, and were, in many cases, outrightly sympathetic with the cause of American independence.

Perhaps it is not unfair to imagine that a direct process of reasoning, from the principles of John Locke to the text of the Declaration, went through the mind of Thomas Jefferson during the last days of June in 1776. For that document begins with a statement of the need to set up a new community, a statement that derives directly from Locke's Essay. It continues with a statement of the rights of man which could not have been worded before Locke's new definiton of the nature of man. It goes on to the long catalogue of the offenses of George III against the rights of free citizens. It closes with an appeal for the support of God for the new community established "in the name and by the authority of the good people of these colonies."

In this document, the new dream of mankind, the vision based on the concept of a society of free men, and rooted in a new philosophic view of man's nature, was given political expression. In it is represented the culmination of the revolution in man's thinking about himself and his world that marked the long transition from the medieval to the modern era.

Just as the Declaration put into definite form for the new

nation the political implications of Locke's thinking, so did the Constitution specify the organs of government by which these implications could be worked out in practice. There is more of Locke's essay on government woven into the fabric of the Constitution than most of us realize.

Take first Locke's three main "wants" of the state of nature, lack of "a settled, known law, of an indifferent judge, and of power in back of the law and the judge." It is easy to see how the need for making good these three lacks meant the setting up of three main branches of government—legislative, judiciary, and executive. Such a pattern was not new. But Locke had given it a new impetus, and a clearer basis.

We should also recall that, according to Locke, men, in setting up a political community, relinquish to it two powers. The first, which we might describe as that of being "a law unto himself," he gives up only to the degree necessary for the preservation of the community. The second, that of punishing those who offend against him, he gives up completely. It is thus natural that the Constitution provides first for the organization of the lawmaking branch of the government, and limits most carefully the powers given to it. To it is given the power to set up a body of settled, known laws that limit the natural freedom of the individual. But the purpose of these laws is to render more secure the enjoyment of the unalienable rights of the individuals of the community who are equally subject to them. Thus, the Constitution, after outlining a framework for the legislative branch of the government, and after exactly specifying the powers that branch shall have, concerns itself with the limitation of the powers of this branch.

In this connection, we should remember the fierce opposition to the acceptance of the Constitution which came from so many who were afraid it might give to the Federal government excessive, even tyrannical, power. Soon after its promulgation, a Bill of Rights, in the form of ten amendments, was added to it. These reactions can be better understood if we see them as the logical result of the wide, if not always conscious, acceptance of Locke's political theories.

The second power that the citizen gives up to the community, that of punishing those who offend against him, he gives up completely. Perhaps that is why, in setting up a court system, and defining its powers, the Constitution does not concern itself to any great extent with the limitation of those powers. In fact, we have here a sort of philosophic ground for the privileged position of our Supreme Court. We have come to regard it as the defender of our Constitutional liberties, and to count upon it to declare unconstitutional any laws which infringe upon those liberties more than absolutely necessary for the purpose of giving the individual greater security than he would otherwise enjoy.

As for the executive power, that which carries out the will of the people, as expressed in the laws of the community, here, too, there is a careful listing of the powers that are granted. Jefferson, and his contemporaries, probably did not foresee the great and increasing measure of power which the President would acquire.

All this detailed consideration of the degree to which Locke's political principles shaped the ideals and institutions of our nation has brought out very clearly one important implication. You may not have noticed it fully, but that old, basic *regret* that governments are necessary haunts all of the agreements which organized our own. If only men could remain in the state of nature! But, since an unfortunate need for government exists, let us have the minimum necessary for the purpose of overcoming our main "wants" of the natural state. Let us be constantly on guard against any attempt on the part of the government to extend its powers beyond that minimum.

Nor is this based upon mere theorizing about typical American attitudes. For proof, we can turn again to Ralph Waldo Emerson, who said, "The less government the better!" Or we can recall the amazing irritation of Thoreau at the mild restraints placed upon him by the town of Concord, and his insistence—which landed him briefly in jail—that he should decide whether or not to pay his taxes. This characteristic attitude of impatience with even mild governmental restraint was greatly strengthened by John Stuart Mill's influential essay *On Liberty*.

All this is of tremendous importance for the understanding of the traditional American attitude towards government in general. Scratch any 100 per cent American, and you will find a man intolerant of any but the minimum interference by government in his life, his business, or his behavior. Only recently and reluctantly have we accepted the need for some regulation of business by our government. Here, in the background we have been exploring, is the clue to the vehement reaction by so many million Americans to the whole basic philosophy of Franklin Roosevelt's "New Deal." When the instinctive dislike of "undue" interference by government is coupled with the belief that government is not showing due concern for its chief function, the protection of property, the resulting resentment knows no bounds to its bitterness. Especially since so often, and so easily, "property" is taken in the narrow sense of possessions only, instead of in the wider sense in which Locke almost always used it, that of including "life" and "liberty."

Here we have a deep, philosophic ground for the blind rage of the Republican against the "socialistic tendencies" of the New Deal, and for that fierce, almost atavistic resentment in the presence of which many of us have felt sick and ashamed. The apoplectic outburst of the rugged individualist against "that man" was due not only to his annoyance at excess profit taxes, "directives" issued to industry, or interference at the surface level with the conduct of his affairs. It was compounded of all these factors. But, deeper than any of them, so deep as to be wholly unconscious, perhaps, was an instinctive rebellion against basic principles opposed to those according to which he had always directed his living and thinking. The principles threatened were that the powers of government should be kept to a minimum, and that the chief function of government should be the protection of "private interests," of "property rights." For the exponents of the New Deal did hold that the common welfare, certainly in time of danger and distress, required a far greater measure of interference by government in the affairs of the land, and that "property rights," especially in such times, must give way to "human rights."

Yet the very real justification for the intrusion of such "foreign ideology" in time of depression was soon forgotten even by many who benefitted from it at the time. The Lockean heritage of traditionally American ideas reasserted itself promptly. Remember the Congressmen who posed at the Capitol in 1946 with brooms, ready to sweep away the last remains of the New Deal? The wish to sweep them away was there, but most of the New Deal "reforms" have remained, and are supported by both political parties.

Another result of this traditional heritage forms a part of the basis for the feeling of discomfort, if not of alarm, which so many Americans have in discussions about the United Nations today. No matter how convinced they may be, in the logical part of their minds, that a strong international system is necessary, they still react unfavorably to the idea of another "layer" of government above them. Then, too, the United Nations is pledged to stress the protection of "human" rather than "property" rights. Small wonder that Americans always have to be reassured that no "Superstate" is really intended by the United Nations. In a large measure, this explains our logical acceptance of the U.N., and our still persistent emotional antipathy toward it. Of course, any great and powerful nation is reluctant to give any international system real power over it. In our case, the additional factors we have been discussing add to our dislike of any real "submission" to international control.

The basic belief that the individual is more important than the state, that touchstone of the faith of the western, democratic world, has other roots than those that draw their nourishment from Locke's philosophy. We should recall the main ones here. For we are dealing here with the deepest tradition that unites men of those nations which, like our own, always profess, and sometimes practice, "political democracy" of the type we have been describing. It is this tradition which is, as we shall see, diametrically opposed by that of the "totalitarian" view which holds that the state is more important than the individual.

Indeed, the "Individualism" of the western world has many roots. Far back, it drew some of its early strength from Rome, which upheld the dignity of the Roman Citizen, and gave to him many of the legal rights which we still insist upon. And it is most important to note that, with the exception of Scandinavia, where freedom is deeply rooted, it is only in those areas of Europe long subject to the rule of Rome that the tradition of freedom has flourished. It, like the armies of Rome, never penetrated very successfully east of the Rhine. A strong "Individualism" seems to have been natural for the peoples of the Atlantic littoral of Europe—especially the Scandinavians, English, Dutch, and the French. Also, the Renaissance and the Reformation contributed their share of Individualism to the development of western Europe. Both played an important part in engendering that healthy skepticism that has traditionally and persistently opposed both political and religious dogmatism and that is by its very nature and of itself a strong and continuing bulwark against communism.

But there are many reasons why Locke has loomed large among these influences that have molded the "Individualism" of the United States, and why his influence so determined the growth of our traditional attitudes and prejudices. In the first place, as we noted, the Declaration and the Constitution were founded four-square on his political theories. In the second place, the opportunities offered by the development of a virgin continent were perfect for the realization of the sort of in- dividualistic Utopia that could be based on Locke's concept of the nature of man. There might well never have been such a country as our own unless Locke's philosophy and political theories had permeated the leaders among those who were conquering and colonizing a vast new world of unlimited promise.

Furthermore, Locke's influence has been not only more definitive but also more persistent among us than elsewhere. In recent times our nation has been less subject to the tensions and pressures that have brought "Individualism" into question in many other areas where it formerly dominated political and social thinking. Under the strain of war and the pressure of privation, England did turn to a socialist pattern of national organization. Most of the nations of western Europe have found it necessary to put increased restraint upon the individual citizen. But in the United States faith in the principles of in- dividualism remains firm and fervid despite world wars and periods of economic collapse. In all honesty it must be ac- knowledged that profession of this faith is not always sufficient to ensure practices and procedures that really foster freedom. We shall see how we all too often betray our own deepest tra- ditions in this respect.

Though this happens, it is nevertheless true that, despite all our difficulties of economic and social adjustment, we are still a nation with immeasurably greater opportunities for the individual than exist in most other lands. But it is also because of the persistence of an underlying philosophy which we absorb in a hundred different ways.

How? Certainly very few of us have studied Locke. But most of us are made familiar with the Declaration of Independence, and are given a warm feeling of emotional allegiance to its principles at an early age. The values we learn at home, at school, at play, are almost always related to the philosophy of the prime importance of the individual. We admire the self-made man. (In Russia the similar object of admiration is the man who has "helped the State.") We are taught to respect the opinion of others. (In Russia there is only One Truth—that handed down from the decisions of The Party.) Even in our childhood games we use the principle of majority decision. We dislike rank and title. We most willingly accept control by local government in which we feel the most direct sense of participation. We are quick to resent interference in our lives. In fact, there is no end to the list of simple, homely examples of the myriad ways in which our philosophic heritage nourishes our individualism.

The establishment of the United States marked the completion, and translation into political terms, of man's revolt against the medieval world. Among the nations of the earth, there was now one founded firmly on the basis of the new, "modern," view of the nature of the world and of man. Because of that, our nation became, and has remained, Utopia for those who believed in the dream of personal freedom, the second great dream of which we spoke as we began this inquiry. Although there is no longer a new continent to develop along with the dream, the dream persists. For there is more space in a dream than in a continent.

"America is a Utopia," said the Mexican, Alfonso Reyes, many years ago. "Before being discovered, America was presented in the dreams of the poets and the investigations of the scientists." Since these poets and scientists were European, the present political and social reality which is the United States had its origins deep in the past of European thought. We must never forget that we are what we are, first of all, because the peoples of Europe dared to dream of a better world. As far back as Platos' *New Atlantis* we find that prescient, if mystic, vision of a better world across the western ocean. It occurred as part of the folk-lore of almost all the peoples of the western outposts of Europe, as a lost continent, a blessed isle. This vision fired the imagination of the earliest explorers, potent as the lust for gold. The United States became its political expression.

But now we must face a new problem. If it was true that for most of our "Founding Fathers" the principle of "the less government the better" seemed basic, how did it come about that our Federal Constitution was ever adopted? First of all, because of the terrible danger in which the new nation stood so long as it was integrated only by the loose Articles of Confederation. Many of our early statesmen felt that it would be almost a miracle if the rich new land were not to be attacked by one of the giants of the European world. Indeed, if England and France had not been so absorbed in fighting each other, the story of the attainment and maintenance of our independence might well have been different. Yet their almost constant warfare during our early years was itself a threat to our security. Unless we were to knit together the semi-autonomous states more closely, attack from abroad, or strife from within, would sooner or later undermine our independence. Even that thoroughgoing Lockean, Thomas Jefferson, came to accept the Federal principle so strongly urged by Hamilton, Jay, and Washington.

But there was an influence which added its weight to the all too apparent dangers of disunity. That was, we now can see, the heritage brought by some of those Englishmen who were most thoroughly permeated by the doctrine and traditions of the Church of England. For this body, though long divorced from the authority of Rome, still maintained a great deal of the point of view of medieval Catholicism. It looked with more favor than did Locke on the idea of a "social" as well as a churchly hierarchy. It had also much more respect for "organic" unity than did the other Protestant sects. In other words, it retained something of the Aristotelian world picture. In the personal and political rivalry between Jefferson and Hamilton, the Lockean and Aristotelian viewpoints were in conflict. Our

Constitution is a resulting compromise, although it leans far more to the Lockean view.

Many authorities feel that the Federal principle—that the Union should come first, should be more important than the States—was not deeply understood nor definitely established until the Civil War. As a result of that tragic struggle it was written on the American consciousness in letters of blood. But, also as a result of the same struggle, as if in compensation, the Lockean doctrine of the real freedom and equality of *all* men was finally extended to the Negroes—at least in theory.

Of course, that extension had always been implicit in the doctrine; Thomas Jefferson had seen that. Deeply troubled, he wrote, in words now engraved on his Memorial in Washington, "I tremble for my country when I reflect that God is just and that His justice cannot sleep forever. Commerce between master and slave is despotism. Nothing is more certainly written in the book of fate than that these people are to be free."

It is interesting and important to note that Jefferson, so well aware of the implications of Locke's philosophy, saw that the existence of slavery would bring dissent and distress. We can only wonder if he foresaw that its end would not bring to all men the equality that he held was theirs by nature.

Now we must turn our attention to some other, secondary factors in the American "way of life." These are economic rather than political in their nature. But they, too, are rooted in philosophy. Before we examine them, we must go back to some developments in British philosophy among those thinkers who followed John Locke.

For Locke, you will remember, there were no "innate" ideas of any kind, and, indeed, no ideas could arise until the mind, the "mental substance," was acted on by the material substances around it. In its reception of "simple" ideas, based on simple sense data, the mind, according to Locke, is "wholly passive." It becomes active only in combining these simple ideas into complex ones, and into general concepts—like red-

ness, loudness, matter, etc. But, Locke also said, "*no* idea can
arise in any human mind until the material substances of the
person's body act on that mind." If this is so, how can we ever
really get to general concepts like those just mentioned? How
can we ever have any knowledge of "relations" like cause and
effect, or any other general laws? How could Newton ever have
worked out the basic laws of the behavior of the universe?

These questions troubled Locke's followers. One, George
Berkeley, Bishop of Cloyne, in Ireland, who lived for a time
in Newport, Rhode Island, came to the conclusion that all our
knowledge of matter, space, time, everything except our immediately sensed "ideas," was mere speculation. We could be
sure of nothing outside of our own immediate ideas. "To be is
to be perceived" was Berkeley's famous definition of reality.

This may itself seem unrealistic. But, on the basis of the
belief that all ideas come from sensation alone, just try to prove
that you can *know* that anything really exists outside of those
ideas! Samuel Johnson thought he could prove the existence
of matter by kicking at a stone. But all he really proved was
that he got a sensation, very painful no doubt, which gave him
an *idea* of the stone. That was all he really *knew*. If matter did
exist outside of his idea of it, he could not get at its real nature.

Berkeley, however, did believe in the existence of *mind,*
though he did not think you could prove the existence of
matter. He was sure, as René Descartes had been, that one
could at least be certain, on the basis of observable evidence,
of the process of thought, and thus of the reality of mind.

Then came David Hume, the skeptical Scotsman, philosopher, and historian. Hume went Berkeley one better. If we
have no right to form any general concepts about matter, he
said, it also follows that we have no right to form any such
concepts about mind. The logical development of Locke's
theories should lead us, Hume held, to the view that all we
can really know is a stream of sense data, a kaleidoscope of
impressions, and of the fleeting associations that accompany

them, such as feelings of like, dislike, pleasure, and pain. Hume denied to the mind the limited activity which Locke had granted it; he made of it a wholly passive thing, the mere camera-like recorder of impressions.

Thus, with Hume, philosophy reached a sort of dead end. Speculation as to the true nature of the world, and of man, was blocked by this devastating conclusion that all we *know* is a stream of sense impressions, and the fleeting feelings connected with them. For a long time thereafter British philosophy remained thus blocked. Eventually the German philosophers, to whom we shall turn for the background of Marxism, showed the way out of this impasse.

It was necessary for us to take account of this frustrating development in British thought because it had a profound effect on economic theories. By way of such theories, it had a definitive effect on the development of our typical attitudes and prejudices here in America. Hume was second only to Locke among the philosophers whose thinking helped to shape the American way of life.

Hume died in the year our Declaration of Independence was born. Thus his influence upon us came later than that of Locke. It came, as a matter of fact, just at the time when the world was beginning to be profoundly changed by the roar, smoke, and bustle of the Industrial Revolution. At first, almost all of this new development, and of its drastic effect on the patterns of men's lives, was confined to England. Thus England had not only the first mills, and the first millionaires, but the first "economic philosophers."

In this period in England, the hold and the tradition of Locke's view of the nature of the human being was strong. This view provided an excellent philosophic ground for taking advantage of the unprecedented opportunities for material gain, for the pursuit of happiness through possessions, which the Industrial Revolution made possible for some fortunate individuals. But the appalling living conditions of most workers, the immense differences in wealth, the exploitation of human lives, and the disregard for human values, which characterized the early years of the capitalist era, demanded some sort of "moral justification."

Hume's philosophical ideas were found to contain a ground for a theory which would provide such a justification—or at least so it seemed. If all that is "really real" for us is a stream of sense impressions, and the associations and feelings that come with them, it is in those associations and feelings that "values" must be found, and a system of good and bad located. It was natural to assume that pleasant feelings were good, and unpleasant ones bad. And so economics must concern itself with the ways in which the pleasant feelings could be increased, and the economists found that such increase was bound up in the satisfaction of our wants. Jevons, one of the leading British economists, in writing of the goal of the new science of economics, said it was "To satisfy our wants to the utmost with the least effort—in other words, *to maximize pleasure.*" With such a goal in mind, it was natural that the early economic philosophers should work out a "pleasure theory of value," in which the worth of any article is determined by the amount and kind of pleasure it can give.

The new types of production, made possible by the new machines, could create an infinitely greater quantity of a great many goods which satisfied men's wants, and which, therefore, should increase men's pleasure—clothes, shoes, tools, building materials. In the excitement of the "new age" there was little room for doubt that man would be happier as a result of all this, and there was, therefore, a philosophic as well as a material ground for the development of the "laissez-faire" theory of economics—the theory that private enterprise should be given free rein. This would result in the greatest production of goods, and such production, in turn, would ultimately result in what John Stuart Mill called "the greatest happiness for the greatest number." The evils of the new industrial system were to be looked upon as temporary only.

Thus here, in the application of the philosophy of Hume to the science of economics, you get the counterpart of the application of the philosophy of Locke to political science. Both gave nourishment to the development of the "Individualistic" point of view. Note that Locke's political premise of "the least government possible," with its resulting prejudice against "interference" by the state in the affairs of its people, was a perfect setting for a "laissez-faire" economy.

After our Civil War, when unprecedented economic opportunities came with the opening up of the whole sweep of the continent, it was the economic motives which played the larger part in the maintenance of the typical American attitudes towards "interference" by government. These motives, along with our traditional political attitudes, made up that bitter resentment against the New Deal of which we have spoken. Today, defense of the American "way of life" is far too largely tied up with the doctrine of free enterprise, and far too little with the doctrine that holds the individual more sacred than the state on deeper philosophic grounds.

During the whole of the nineteenth century, our nation was busy with the exploration, settlement, and development of its broad sweep from sea to sea. The economically displaced of Europe's poor were pouring into it in the hope of a better life, and were providing a cheap supply of labor. The frontier of civilization and of human hope marched westward together across the United States. For us, therefore, there was little cause to turn to other philosophic bases for political or economic theory. The bases that Locke and Hume had given us were still satisfactory for life in a land of swift growth and marvelous opportunities. What new influences of importance there were came from new champions of liberty such as John Stuart Mill, whose masterly defense of freedom of opinion,

and of speech, was widely effective, and from our own in-
dividualists, like Emerson and Thoreau. New social and
economic theories made little if any impact on us; we were too
busy, and we lacked the background of new philosophic speculation in which such theories were based.

But elsewhere in the world an upheaval in philosophy, and
it resulting groundswell of new social theory, were shaking
the foundations of the form of a "free society"— one such as
our own. Unperceived at the time, they were also preparing
the bases for those systems of totalitarianism, of state control
of the whole life of a nation, which are in conflict with us in
these later years.

6

The Roots of Marxism—
Man as the Power of Will

WE MUST now turn to the difficult field of German Idealism, which must be understood to understand Marxism. For it was in the German philosophers of the late eighteenth and early nineteenth centuries, in their theories as to the nature of the world, and of man, that the doctrines of Karl Marx had their roots. He could not have developed those ideas of man, society, and the state, which have so shaken the world, had the course of speculation in Germany been otherwise than it was.

Not only are the basic concepts of these German thinkers difficult. They are almost completely unfamiliar to most of us. Our background of philosophic ideas, so largely drawn from Locke and Hume, is utterly different, and our whole "frame of reference" for political and social ideas differs accordingly. Especially with regard to theories as to the relation of man to the state, the ideas that underlie Marx's doctrines are so alien to our own as to be their exact opposite. When we pass from our own set of basic concepts to these contrasting ones, we seem to be passing through a sort of theoretical "looking glass" into a region where all ideas and all values are utterly reversed. This is, after all, pretty much what happens today when you pass through the Iron Curtain to the Sovietized world beyond.

We instinctively believe, and with good reason, that there is something terribly wrong about a system that so completely overturns the whole set of personal and political values to which we are accustomed. It *cannot* be right, we feel, that the function of government should be to control the lives, work, and thoughts of all citizens at all times. It *cannot* be right to teach that one political viewpoint and one party is entirely correct, and that all others must be suppressed. But it will do us, and the world, no good if, when we are confronted with such views, we react merely with anger, or despair. There is, there *must* be, a reason why such views exist. In so far as that reason is rooted in philosophy we must now undertake to uncover it. A full understanding of the basic causes of the diametrically opposed points of view of the West and of the Soviet Union requires such an inquiry. No examination or comparisons at the surface level of political and social theory will suffice.

Locke, on the basis of Newton's world picture, had given a definition of the nature of man and principles for the organization of civil society which seemed clear, logical, and satisfactory to the founders of our nation. We have discussed at length the reasons why these bases have remained satisfactory for us, and the factors that have furthered this persistence. It was not, however, only because such factors—a frontier to develop, incomparable resources, technical skills, etc.—were lacking in Europe that a new revolution against our idea of a "free society" began there. This new revolution, which was given its "Declaration of Independence" by Marx, and its "Constitution" by Lenin, was rooted not only in nineteenth-century economic distress but in eighteenth-century philosophy. Had Locke's basic doctrines continued to satisfy the philosophers of the continent, as well as those of England, we should probably never have heard of National Socialism or the Communism of Karl Marx.

The revolution in philosophy which produced those concepts of man, the world, and the state, on which modern totalitarianism is based, began in the mind of an obscure little professor in East Prussia. Immanuel Kant was born in Königsberg in 1724, died there in 1804—just one hundred years after Locke—and may well never have gone more than a day's journey away from there during his entire life. But his mind traveled over reaches vaster than the universe, and he gave to philosophy a whole new approach to its perennial problems.

That new approach was sorely needed. As we noted, David Hume had landed philosophy in a dead-end street from which there seemed to be no escape. If all we could know was a stream of sense impressions, and the feelings associated with them, what was the use of attempting any real knowledge of the actual nature of our world?

Metaphysical inquiry, however, is like love. If one way of approach to the beloved is blocked, it will find another. The mind of man plays, and has always played, as Plato said, the part of the lover seeking Truth as its Beloved.

Kant, therefore, realized that there must be a new attack on the stronghold of true knowledge of our world. Hume, said Kant, awoke him from his "dogmatic slumbers." Could Hume have been wrong? Was there some way in which we could be sure of knowing more than a stream of sense impressions? Well, not so long as we concentrate our attention on the nature of what we actually perceive. So long as we do that, we can only define and redefine the impressions we get through our senses. We can never get to any knowledge of what the stimuli to our sensations are like in themselves. Hume was correct also in showing that, by using this approach only, we have no right to general concepts of any kind. We are still left with a stream of impressions as all we can really know.

But, in such a view, the mind is only the passive receiver of sense impressions. It does not show spontaneous activity of its own; it is merely acted upon by material substances in the body or outside. Locke had held that the mind *was* active in forming complex ideas, and general concepts, out of simple ideas. Hume had done away with even such limited activity. Right here Kant found a clue, one which was to lead him out of the dead end. Was the mind really such a wholly passive thing? Was it merely a "blank tablet" at birth? In other words, Kant set himself to examine the nature of the *mind* rather than the nature of the impressions it got from outside itself. He wanted to find out if he could prove that it was active, and whether or not it had any knowledge that did not depend on sense experience.

Let us take an example of the sort of consideration that drove Kant to think the mind must be active and that it might well have knowledge not directly dependent on sense. The example is that of our firm conviction that there is a law of "cause and effect," a law on which everyone depends, a law on which Newton had hung his universe, a law which says that the same causes will produce the same effects.

According to Hume, we have no right to assume such a "law." We can merely *hope* that a pattern of sense impressions we note today, that thunder follows lightning, let's say, will repeat itself tomorrow. But we cannot be certain; we cannot *know* that lightning will always cause thunder, whether or not we are near enough to hear it.

This just won't do. We are all certain that such general laws as that of cause and effect do exist; we order our lives on such a certainty; indeed, on it Newton based his whole world picture. But how can we be certain? Hume was right in pointing out that we cannot get to that certainty by sense impressions.

Kant's answer was that we were thus certain, that we could comprehend such general laws, *because of the nature of the human mind itself*. It is true that the *content* of our minds is filled in by experience, and that the content of each man's mind is determined by the record that experience writes upon it. But Locke had given only a partial representation of the mind, in his "blank tablet" figure of speech. What he had failed to bring out was that the *methods* of receiving impressions on those tablets were always constant. Being as they are by nature, they have to receive the impressions of sense in certain ways. Also, in their receiving of such impressions they are active, not "wholly passive" at all. As impressions strike the mind, they are not only recorded, but arranged in a certain manner, in terms of certain characteristics of the human mind, of which that of grasping impressions in terms of the law of cause and effect is one.

If this were not so, there would be no uniformity to the general character of the record of sense experience in different minds. Kant's great achievement was to prove that there is another factor in the process of *knowing*. This process is not merely one of passively receiving impressions; there is also involved in it an active shaping of those impressions in the very process of receiving them.

This is the reason that knowledge takes the same *form* with all men, no matter how different its specific *content* may be. It is also the reason why knowledge is transferable, why education is possible. The basic framework of all minds is the same, no matter how differently that framework is filled in, or ornamented. This basic framework determines that all minds *must* know things as located in space and time, and as related to each other in constant and dependable patterns, such as that of cause and effect. This Kant called *a priori* knowledge, which means merely knowledge "from before," rather than after, sense data.

By this profound bit of insight, Kant re-established the

prestige of the human mind. For Kant, the mind was both the receiver of sense impressions, and, simultaneously, their arranger into patterns that are meaningful for all men. This is true, we should note, not only in the case of general laws of the behavior of things. It is true for our knowledge of all things. An artist could not *know* that when he mixes blue and yellow he will always get green, unless his mind added to his impressions of colors a sure conviction that those two will always interact in the same way. A musician could not foresee that a violin string twice as long as another would always produce a pitch just so much deeper unless he had a similar sure conviction of regularity of relation. These calculations seem simple enough, but they represent exactly the same sort of mental activity which enables an astronomer to know, centuries in advance, how the stars will swing through space throughout all time. In all such cases something is added by the active mind that no amount of mere *observance* of sense data could supply.

This account of the way in which Kant rescued philosophic speculation from the impasse Hume had led it into brings us at once to a most important point. To the German philosophers on whom Marx based his theories, to Kant himself, and to his followers, the whole philosophic foundations of the "free society" of the western nations were seen as overthrown as early as 1790. They not only found the thinking of Locke and Hume inadequate; they thought of the political and social systems based thereon as inadequate too. The charge made by Hitler and Mussolini, that the whole "culture" of the democratic powers was outmoded, decadent, finished, absurd as history has proved it to be, was based on a philosophic conviction already a century and a half old. But the dictators of Germany and Italy were forgetting, like the leaders of communism today, that the philosophic bases of *their* systems may perhaps also be discredited.

We must now return to Kant's philosophy. The part of it

with which we have been dealing, his theory of the nature of knowledge, provided a basis for discrediting the philosophic foundations of the western, democratic world. For if Locke and Hume had been wrong in their theory of knowledge because of a mistaken concept of the character of the human mind, their interpretation of the nature of the human being was at fault. That meant that the recommendations for political society which Locke had given were not correct, since these were suited only to the human individual as Locke had conceived him. Since Hume had been more thoroughly wrong than Locke in denying *any* activity to the human mind, any theory of economics based on his philosophy was even more incorrect. Therefore the political and social systems of the West were based on inadequate foundations and should be supplanted by new systems.

It was another part of Kant's philosophic theories that provided the foundations for such new systems. Kant was convinced, and convinced the philosophic world, that the mind was an active entity. He divided its activity into three parts— thinking, willing, and feeling. In the first, man seeks a theory of knowledge, in the second, a theory of morals, in the last, a theory of beauty. We need to be concerned only with the first two of these activities of the mind.

In his first great book, *Critique of Pure Reason,* Kant dealt with a theory of knowledge. Perhaps no one was more surprised than he when he found that Pure Reason could not demonstrate any proofs of the *real* existence of things, nor of the soul, immortality, or God. All we could know through the Pure Reason, through the activity of *knowing,* was the *appearance* of things outside us. We could not know what things were like in their own nature. Even though the mind was active in its reception of these appearances, it was limited in its knowledge of them.

Now this was a terrible blow to Kant. For he, even more than Locke, was a profoundly religious man. He felt *sure* of the existence of God. But where did that surety come from if knowledge of the appearances of things did not bring it? Kant found the clue to his answer in the *moral nature* of man, in his capacity to *will* the good, and to resist evil. One of Kant's most famous sayings was, "Two things fill me with awe; the starry heavens above, the moral law within." Kant had no doubt that both were real, real in the sense of having an existence independent of the observer. But, in the case of the stars, we could know them only as they appear to us. In the case of the moral law we could know something as it was "in-itself." Its very home is in our hearts; we see there no mere shadow of its reality.

For Kant, it was this moral sense, this sense of right and wrong, that proved there was freedom of choice in our actions. If such freedom of the will existed, there must be personal immortality, so that good actions should be rewarded, and bad actions punished. There must be a God to approve or disapprove, and to provide an ultimate ground for the sense of right and wrong itself. Thus Kant, in his moral philosophy, as given in his second great work, *Critique of Practical Reason,* found the bases for belief in freedom of the will, the immortal soul, and God, bases which his scientific philosophy had not given him.

Here we come to a point of the utmost importance. Kant's thinking thus led him to put a higher value upon the result of the activity of willing than upon that of knowing. Whether or not he ever acknowledged this, it follows from the fact that through knowing we find only a world of appearances, the real nature of which we cannot know. But through willing we are at once attuned to the very nature of the world. To Kant, that nature was thoroughly *moral,* and our experience in exercising our will was sure to be moral experience. Nevertheless, the result was to make *will* the most fundamental quality of the human soul.

Will was to become the essence of the human being instead

of interpretive *reason,* as it had been for Locke. What characterizes a human being is not to be an independent observer and interpreter of the world. No, his essential character is his ability to will the good, to be an active, striving, willful "self."

Right here is the beginning of the very different concepts of the nature, and proper *function,* of the individual which underlie the totalitarian attitudes. If the philosophy on which your political thinking is based is rooted largely in Locke, you think of man as the rational observer and interpreter of the world. This means that each individual should have the greatest possible freedom of observation and interpretation, in order that the sum total of human knowledge may be increased by all differing experience. But, if your political thinking has its roots in Kant, and in his followers, you think of man as primarily an agent of the *will,* as the focus of a force which decides, changes, opposes. This means that the individual must submit himself to a stern inner moral law, as it did for Kant, or that he must submit himself to the authority of something larger than himself—the State, which is a more effective agent of The Will than he alone can be. This is perhaps not entirely clear, but we shall see how it develops, as we move on to the thinking of those who followed Kant.

The two German thinkers responsible for the further developments of Kant's ideas with which we are concerned were Johann Gottlieb Fichte, who lived from 1762 to 1814, and Georg Wilhelm Friedrich Hegel, whose dates were from 1770 to 1831. It was their philosophic systems, especially that of Hegel, from which Karl Marx drew his political and social ideas. We had better deal first with Fichte, who was a professor of philosophy at several German universities, longest at Jena and Berlin.

Kant had made a distinction between man as *knower* of the physical world, and man as *willer* of the good. When Fichte read Kant's works, in 1790, he did not like that distinction; he wanted to characterize man in *one* way, and to assign to him *one* essential function. He thought he saw how this could be done. *All* our knowledge, he held, knowledge of the physical world as well as of good and evil, depends upon an *act of will.* Without such an act we could have no knowledge. True, we observe a stream of sense experience, and our minds supply some elements in the act of knowing, much as Kant had said. We also develop certain theories to explain what we observe. But when we actually choose and accept any such theory we indulge in an act of *will.* Man's distinguishing function is thus to exercise his will even in the process of knowing his world.

This may seem surprising at first. But, thus far, Fichte's theory has nothing dangerous about it, and, in fact, would be accepted generally by most modern scientists. It is quite true that in our attempts to explain the nature of the physical world we "choose a theory," develop a hypothesis, that is, and then retain it if what we observe confirms it. Otherwise, we drop it and choose another. Even in "exact" science there is an exercise of the will in this sense. Our knowledge *does* involve an act of will.

There is, however, a grave danger in stressing *will* as the fundamental activity of man. So long as that will is exerted to overcome ignorance, or to overcome evil, all is well. For man alone is capable of directing this quality of will, which he shares with all animal life, perhaps with all living things, to such noble ends.

But, to an alarming extent, Fichte and his followers thought of the exercise of will as so much the nature and function of man that the ends to which it is put became of lessening importance. To will, to struggle, to overcome, became the hallmark of humanity. We of today's world are well able to assess the terrible evil which has resulted from directing will toward *power* instead of *good.*

We must investigate how Fichte developed this idea in such a way that it began to have dangerous implications for political doctrines. Since his interpretation of the nature of man puts a premium on men's ability to *will* things, strong, dominant individuals, those in whom the exercise of the will is most vigorous, could convince others to follow them by insisting that their willfulness entitled them to be leaders. For, as Northrop says, Fichte's approach to the nature of man leads to a view which "identifies the good life not with the fact that . . . all men are . . . politically equal, but with the degree to which the individual gives expression to his own will."

Fichte, like Locke, talked about "natural rights," but he had a very different concept of their nature, and of the claim man had upon them. This claim of the individual for freedom of his person, and protection of his property, rested, for Fichte, upon its being necessary for the individual to have this freedom and this protection "for the performance of duty." For Locke, there had been no such contingent necessity, the rights had been absolute, "unalienable." For Fichte, they are enjoyed only so that man may do his duty. At this point, we must ask, his duty to what?

The answer is, to The State! Right here we can see how Fichte's thinking is tending in a dangerous direction. Kant would have said that man's duty was to the Moral Law which he would find in his own heart, not primarily in the laws of his state, for these were mere approximations of the Moral Law. But Fichte found it natural to see in the organization of The State a focus of the will far more effective than a mere individual. Because The State could exercise will better than an individual it was worthy of his submission to it. Therefore, it was natural for Fichte to make man's rights dependent on his performance of his duty to The State.

For Locke, the state was a regrettable necessity to the organization of which men turned the better to safeguard their individual lives, liberties, and properties. For Fichte, the state was a desirable means for the more efficient performance of man's essential function, the expression and exercise of will. One view was based on a concept of man as observer and interpreter of the world, a concept compatible with a maximum of liberty for each individual. The other was a view based on a different concept of man, as a storm center of will, one which was to make it natural to disparage independence of the individual in favor of the state as a more effective focus for the will.

We must deal a bit more with this basic concept of Fichte, the primacy of the will. If man's nature, his *self,* is characterized so essentially as a center of the will, his primary function, Fichte held, must be to express this nature by *overcoming* something outside himself—the "not-self." Each individual carries on this all-pervasive struggle. But over, above, around us all is an Absolute Will. As individuals, we can accomplish only a very limited amount in that struggle. But we can believe that the Absolute Will can accomplish anything it wants to. It follows that we, as little auxiliary power stations of the same force, should help it all we can. Beginning with Fichte, but really developed by Hegel, was the idea that we should identify our own wills with that of a larger and more effective power station, the state. We shall see how Hegel worked this out.

First, however, we should note that we are dealing here with a doctrine that reminds us in one way of the world view of Aristotle. Here again we have the idea of the human individual as aware of a purpose in the world, and of being under the obligation to help it fulfill itself. But, in the case of Fichte and Hegel, this obligation was seen as operating in the relation between the individual and the state. In the medieval view it was seen as operating in the field of religion. The identification of the will of the individual with that of God is not unfamiliar to us, nor is the idea of finding our real "freedom" in doing so. Some of us know by heart the creed which says, "In His service is perfect freedom." But we have never accepted the idea that the individual is under such obligation to the state, nor, certainly, that he can find "freedom" by submitting his will to that of the state. To us, that sounds like the most outrageous nonsense.

One more point about Fichte should be mentioned, for we shall refer to it in our conclusions. Not only did his thinking tend towards supplying the bases for totalitarianism in general; he also gave the grounds for German nationalism in a most specific form. A few quotations from his famous *Addresses to the German Nation* will make this frighteningly clear.

Fichte stated that the German is a "primitive" man, and really has a *nation* because his part of Europe was never over-run and ruined by Rome, as western Europe had been. In fact, Fichte exults that the Romans had never conquered the German tribes. If they had, he cried, "then the entire future development of mankind would have taken a direction we cannot imagine would have been more pleasant." *Who* cannot imagine, we may ask? Obviously, the Germans themselves. Anyone else, certainly, with the raw record of history before him, realizes how very much "pleasanter" that record might have been if the Germans had had some centuries of the civilizing effects of Roman rule.

Fichte went on to say, "A true German can wish to live only that he may be and remain forever a German, and may train all that belong to him to be Germans." Be sure to note that "all that belong to him." What would have been wrong for Rome, or for the armies of Napoleon then threatening Germany, to do—overrun and "train" the Germans—is not only right but a *duty* for the Germans themselves. There was a sturdy and continuous line of development right from Fichte to Nazism.

This is true, especially, since Fichte, like Hitler, thought of Germany as the savior of humanity. To the Germans of his day, Fichte said, "If you perish as a nation all the hope of the entire human race for rescue from the depths of its woe perishes together with you—if you sink, all humanity sinks with you, devoid of any hope of restoration at any future time."

It is true that the specific and immediate purpose of Fichte's *Addresses* was to exhort the German people of his time to resist Napoleon, and to do so in the name of "Freedom." But the point of view shown in the quotations given was not merely absurd, as it appears to us to be. It held within it a danger for the world which has been realized in our own times. The *Addresses* became one of the most powerful influences in the development of that militant German spirit which has twice devastated our world. It became, also, an element in the basic philosophy of the totalitarian state. It combined rampant and jingoistic patriotism with the concept of the state as commanding the unquestioning allegiance of the individual on philosophic grounds.

We shall do well to recall here the arrogant certainty of so many Germans that their nation is, as a matter of indisputable fact, superior to all others. This certainty has one of its most important roots in Fichte's works. Another draws its nourishment from Hegel's rating of the German state as the best form of government. Most of us have known Germans to whom this superiority seemed beyond question. The *Kultur* of their nation, by which they mean not only its intellectual and artistic life, but its scientific achievements and its political and social forms, is the best that history had produced. It seems to many Germans a sort of *moral necessity* that their nation should rule the world. Much the same attitude invests the behavior of Soviet Russia today, as we shall see, and it is drawn from the same philosophic sources. We, with our totally different philosophic conditioning, have no such imperious conviction that we should rule the world.

We should remember here that Fichte and Hegel were by no means the only main sources of the "will to aggression" of the modern German state. Beginning with Schopenhauer, a contemporary of Hegel, there had been an important strain in German thought which had taken up and further developed the concept that the will is the all-decisive factor in man's role on earth. Schopenhauer himself taught that restraint of will was man's duty. Others who followed him, however, glorified the uninhibited exercise of will, and Nietzsche, the direct progenitor of Nazi thought, held that only through this could man transcend his present limitations and become Superman. All the merciful restraints of Christian morality were to be cast aside, and the ideal was to be the "blond beast" who knew no law or code of morals except that of his own strength. We have seen all too clearly what this cult has done to our world. We may not have realized, however, the deeper and more reputable sources of the spirit of aggression which the Germans derived from Fichte, and, as we shall see, from Hegel as well.

We are now getting close to the world picture which formed the background for the theories of Marx, and for the political and social institutions of Soviet Russia. But that picture will not present itself clearly until we have taken a frightening look at the philosophy of Fichte's successor as Germany's first thinker—G. W. F. Hegel.

In the writings of Hegel, who became the high priest of German philosophy, these concepts of the nature of man, and of his relation of the state, take on forms in which we can clearly see the bases for the theory of the Totalitarian State. Hegel wrote about all matters. His "System," which won the awe and admiration of the philosophic world, explains absolutely everything—logic, psychology, law, ethics, government, art, religion, anything you want will be found in this vast exposition of philosophy. The System is complete, logical, consistent. The difficulties begin only when you try to make it square with man's direct and real experience of the world that he lives in. Simone de Beauvoir, the Existentialist, writes that during the German occupation of Paris she sometimes found comfort by retreating to a library and reading Hegel. But, when she emerged into the streets and life of her captive Paris, that comfort was of no avail. There are many others who have had similar experience with Hegel's work. It is impressive

to anyone. But it does not carry much conviction with it unless
you accept certain premises which may well not be so securely
founded as Hegel held them to be.

For Hegel, the "Will" of Fichte is supplanted by "The Idea."
By this he did not mean what Plato meant by this word, an
unchanging archetypal form of which all actual instances on
earth were imperfect copies. No, for him The Idea, or The
Absolute, as he also called it, was something quite otherwise,
something far more inclusive, and far more closely related to
Will in its expression.

Think of this "Absolute Idea" first as a pre-existent blueprint
of the design of our world. Not only of its physical structure
and laws of behavior, but of its rational and moral nature as
Hegel conceived this to be. Then take the universe, and the
sum total of its known and unknown history, as the working
out in concrete reality of this pre-existent plan. Now stretch
your mind a bit further, and think of Hegel's Absolute as being
all of this, both the plan and its realization. Add to this the
somewhat curious notion that the Absolute, as the pre-existent,
a priori plan, translates itself into the world as we find it, and
history as it occurs, in order to contemplate itself, in order
to provide a sort of cosmic looking-glass for itself. Otherwise,
we are led to assume, the restless Absolute would get bored
with itself.

Let us note here that all of this seeming abracadabra is,
perhaps, only a new and unnecessarily difficult way of re-
stating the old medieval, Christian world picture—spirit
becoming matter, "The Word" becoming flesh. There is much
in the Hegelian picture that is similar, but there are important
differences, and dangerous implications, in the later doctrine.
These have to do with the identification of the *state* with the
revelation of the political purposes of the Absolute.

Hegel did this for the following consistent reason. The
Absolute is rational. Therefore, the whole story of world history
must also be rational, since it is the Absolute translating a pre-

existing plan into actuality. Therefore, everything that happens is rational. This led Hegel to the maddening statement, "The real is the rational," that is, that all that has happened in the long, bloody, wasteful record of history is the revelation of a rational plan! Even the modern totalitarian state is part of such a revelation. No wonder it is possible to believe that in Hegel's Absolute there was more of will and less of reason than either its author or his followers fully realized. This seems true particularly of the further developments of the doctrine of Hegel's theory of the state.

As Hegel conceived this theory, it had results of great importance for totalitarian practices, as we shall see. This was made possible by the fact that Hegel, in his development of a theory of government, said, "The State is the Divine Idea as it exists on earth." In other words, the Absolute Idea reveals its rational plan for the *political* welfare of mankind in the form of national organization.

Think about this rather breath-taking statement for a moment. Only by grasping what it really means can you understand the awful power of authority which this concept gives to the totalitarian state, or the ready submission to that authority which marks the people of such states. Their allegiance is given to their state not because it is a convenient institution or an efficient means of improving their lives, but because it represents the revelation of an inspired plan for their betterment. Many millions of Germans, for reasons too complex to recount, were at this time disposed to turn from the community of the Christian faith to the new community of the dynamic, aggressive, all conquering state as the larger whole needed to give meaning to their lives. For such a development, Hegel had given the perfect philosophic ground.

We are here in a totally different political climate from our own. To us, there is something outrageous, something almost terrifying, in the idea of the state as the revelation of a Divine plan. To us, the state isn't a "revelation" of any plan, let alone a Divine one. It is a form of political organization agreed upon, perhaps rather regretfully, by free and equal citizens who find in it a better means of guarding their liberties and protecting their properties than they would otherwise have. Under its aegis, men can better perform their essential rational function of observing and interpreting their world, and can better pursue their happiness.

But when you change your concept of the function of man to that of giving expression to *will,* to the struggle to overcome opposition, then your concept of the function of the state has got to change, too. With such a view of the function of man in mind, it is logical for your view of the state to change as it did with Fichte and Hegel. With the former you reached the idea that the state was a higher and better focus for the function of expressing the will and overcoming opposition than the individual. With the latter you got to the idea that the state has a sort of divine sanction, that man is destined to develop better and better states, and to submit himself to them in order to bring about in actual history the revelation of a pre-existing plan.

All this seems to many of us now a lot of sheer hocus-pocus. Wasn't the view that the world is a revelation of a Divine Plan much better and more simply expressed by the traditional Christian view? That view, as we noted, never identified the development of man's *political* institutions with such a revelation. If you do so, as Hegel did, you give to the state and to its authority a mystic and compelling character which is undeserved, inappropriate, and dangerous in the extreme. No wonder that the indoctrinated citizens of a totalitarian state give to their nation and its leaders a blind devotion; it is the result of a transfer of the religious attitude into the political field. No wonder that Nazism or communism takes the place of religion; it has absorbed the attributes of religion itself. Dogmatic religion poses a threat to freedom, dogmatic "statism" sounds its death knell.

We need not keep to general terms only in examining Hegel's theory of the state. We can turn to some of his specific observations about it. He says that the state should not be founded "as if the individual, in his relations to other individuals, thus limited his freedom in order that this universal limitation—the mutual constraint of all—might secure a small space of liberty for each." This, by the way, is an exact and good description of our traditional basis for forming a state.

Hegel also wrote, "Men are as foolish as to forget . . . in their enthusiasm for liberty of conscience and political freedom, the truth which lies in power." Of this, Ernst Cassirer says, "These words, written in 1801, about 150 years ago, contain the clearest and most ruthless program of fascism that has ever been propounded by any political or philosophic writer." We may note that, as is usual with such philosophic foundations of political action, it took many years for this principle to find its full embodiment in the formation of Hitler's Third Reich.

Hegel denounces as well the theory that man is "free by nature." He says that man can become free by increasing his understanding of what the Divine Idea is revealing—probably by reading Hegel. Man's real "Freedom" does not come from putting the least possible restraint upon the individuals in a political society; it comes only from identifying the individual's will with the Will of the State, the collective will of a nation. Then you are "free" because you, by this identification of your will with that of your state, can overcome so much more opposition. Here is the philosophical root for the Communist definition of "freedom."

This seems to satisfy those who are hypnotized by the totalitarian hypothesis, who feel that the state is of far greater importance than its citizens, and that they can find freedom by merging their wills with its designs. But to us it may seem a mischievous misuse of the good word, Freedom. For is not freedom a quality that has no meaning unless it is an attribute of an individual? At least for us it does not carry the same

color, the same glow, when it is applied to the feeling of ex-
panded personal power that one may get from identifying himself with the state. Perhaps that can be very satisfying if you
think of yourself as primarily a focal point for the expression
of will. It isn't, if you think of yourself as primarily an independent observer and interpreter of the world. It isn't, in
the latter case, what you mean by "freedom" at all.

Hegel, in addition to extolling The State in general terms,
dwells upon the importance of certain "World-Historical
States," of which, of course, Prussia was the current example.
In his *Philosophy of Right* he wrote, "The world spirit, in its
onward march, hands over to each people the task of working
out its own peculiar vocation—each nation in turn is for that
epoch dominant. Against this absolute right to be the bearer of
the development of the world spirit other nations are absolutely
without right."

It is frightening to realize what this opinion has meant in
terms of history. This sanction for ruthless aggression by Germany has stamped the thinking and stilled the conscience of
the Germans ever since. Hegel, who thought of himself as a
Christian, was here giving his philosophic blessing to all the
forthcoming violations by Germany of all principles of Christian morality.

We must note also that Hegel provided for World Historical
Individuals as well as states. Such individuals he regards as
the often unconscious instruments of destiny, and excludes
them from the ranks of those to whom the ordinary codes of
moral behavior apply. Thus, in a passage quoted by Northrop,
he says, "A World-historical individual . . . is devoted to
one aim, regardless of all else. It is even possible that such men
may treat other great, even sacred interests, inconsiderately;
conduct which is indeed obnoxious to moral reprehension,
but so mighty a form must trample down many an innocent
flower—crush to pieces many an object in the path."

Call to mind here Hitler weeping over the ruins of Warsaw

which he was "forced" to destroy because it resisted him, because it stood in "the path." No clearer example of the dangers of such a doctrine need be given. Here is a wellspring of the *Führer-Prinzip,* the doctrine of the Leader who must be blindly obeyed because he is revealing the purposes of destiny. Who can say we have no quarrel with the German people so long as their political theories are founded on such a philosophical heritage? Who can hope to wish away our differences with any totalitarian power which draws its forms and functions from this heritage?

There is one more element of Hegel's philosophy with which we must concern ourselves in this connection. It is one to which we have not yet referred, but it is basic to the whole cosmic fantasy of the Hegelian system, and it became, and has remained, a pivot of Marxist thought. It is the doctrine of the "Dialectic."

Dialectic is an old word in philosophy. It was used to describe the method of argument favored by Socrates, a technique of arriving at truth by reconciling two opposing statements. I make a statement about the nature of man, for example. You make an opposing one. Then we try to reconcile our statements, and distill a better definition out of our conflicting concepts. As a form of logical argument, the dialectical method is good and useful. But Hegel made of it something far more important.

According to Hegel, this dialectic process is not merely a useful pattern for logical argument. It is the pattern by means of which all history proceeds in realizing the plan of the Divine Idea. Each stage of this realization presents a "Thesis." But every thesis brings with it, like a shadow, its opposite or negative, which is called its "Antithesis." Out of the ensuing conflict a "Synthesis" of the two arises, and this, in its turn, becomes a new thesis for a new conflict.

The very essence of history, therefore, is "dialectic," since it progresses only through a series of conflicts and clashes.

Thus did Hegel apply to the very nature of the whole course of history a method of procedure valid in the field of logical argument.

Now all that sounds very complicated, and very unreal. But Hegel thought it was real enough, and, as we shall see, Marx took up the pattern as the one according to which all changes in society occur. For that reason, we must try to understand it fully.

We can take one of Hegel's own examples. The early Roman Republic, a stage in the revelation of the Divine Idea in state form, was a "thesis." Its institutions affirmed a part-truth, that all (free) men should share in the affairs of state. But this carried with it its proper "antithesis" because, under such a system, a few powerful individuals rose to the top (Caesar, Pompey, etc.), and struggled among themselves, asserting another part-truth, that the affairs of state must be disturbed by the rivalry of the most "willful" citizens. But when Caesar put down his rivals, and ruled alone, deciding himself how much share the people should have in government, then a "synthesis" appeared, one which asserted the higher truth that the rule of one leader is better than that of the many, or that of the warring few. Note that Hegel was no believer in democracy; his derivation from Fichte, as well as his belief in the Divine sanction for World-Historical States and Individuals, made this impossible. He held the Prussian monarchy to be the best type of state ever developed.

It is interesting to remember that Bismarck's policies made use of Hegel's ideas about the historic mission of the Prussian State. It was the philosophic ground which Hegel gave him which made Bismarck feel justified in waging the wars which unified the German nation in 1870, and set it on the road to 1914 and 1939.

But we must return to the dialectic. It is extremely hard for us whose philosophic background, unconscious as it may be, is so different, to understand the lure of this theory of the "dialectical nature of history."

But, if you believe that the force of will is the basis of all that occurs, it becomes natural to accept a doctrine which stresses the fundamental importance of *conflict.* If you see all human experience in terms of an endless series of conflicts and overcomings, it is, perhaps, natural to attribute such a pattern to the proceedings of world history. In that case, the dialectic pattern may seem a necessary part of the development of the world, of man, and of man's institutions.

Now let us examine the main building materials once more which Marx was to pick up on his excursion through German philosophy, and use as the bases of his theories. From Fichte, the idea that all our knowledge is a matter of exercising the *will,* that the meaning of our lives is *struggle* and the *overcoming of opposition,* a battle that goes on constantly. Also, that the state, as Fichte conceived it, merits our allegiance, not because it is a convenience for us, but because it is a more efficient focus for the exercise of will than a mere individual can be. Thus, whatever rights man has, he holds in order to serve the state, which should have the power to supervise all his affairs.

Then, from Hegel, Marx got the idea that the state is not only a more efficient focus of the *will* which motivates all things, but that it should be revered as the revelation, in political form, of a Divine plan. Note here that Marx was to substitute the Communist Party for the State as an object of veneration. From Hegel also, the idea that "Freedom" consists in identifying the will of the individual with that of the state. Also, that all of history represents the working out of a rational design so that "all that happens, happens for the best," even though we can't see why. Finally, that history reveals its grim purposes by a three-step routine, the Dialectical Process of Thesis, Antithesis, Synthesis.

Now we must add one more element that influenced Marx's thought. This is to be found in certain modifications of Hegel's ideas made by Ludwig Feuerbach, who lived from 1804 to 1872. He did not have much use for the "Absolute Idea." In fact, he was one of the first to point out that the whole super-colossal edifice of the Hegelian "System" was really a mere restatement of old Christian doctrine.

But for the atheist, Marx, something else that Feuerbach said was of greater importance. Having, in a sense, debunked the Absolute, he went on to give his opinion as to what we find when we seek the real origins of man, and of his world, as they are today. We do not find, said Feuerbach, any pre-existent Absolute Idea. What we find, if mankind is the real object of our study, are the primitive myths, legends, customs, and tabus of early human society. These, developing out of the basic needs of such a society, are the origin of our ideas about the world. We delude ourselves if we believe in a pre-existent Idea, as did Hegel. Thus Feuerbach, though he remained a Christian because of the practical and useful benefits of Christian teachings, called himself a Materialist, one who believes that matter came before mind, instead of an Idealist, one who, like Hegel, believes that mind preceded matter.

Marx seized upon Feuerbach's idea that all our knowledge about the nature of man arises from a study of his *social needs.* Feuerbach had stated specifically that the starting point of any such inquiry should be concerned with man's needs for Production, Reproduction, and Communication. Marx fastened firmly on to the first of these, Production, as being the most important, and put his whole doctrine of history in terms of man's answer to the challenge of meeting adequately his needs for *producing* the essentials of his life—shelter, food, and, later, goods of all kinds.

Here, as we shall see more fully later, are the origins of the doctrine of "Dialectical Materialism" which is the basis for all Marxist teachings. That doctrine is materialistic because it holds that matter, and material concerns, are the ultimate reality; it is dialectic because it holds that history proceeds according to a series of violent conflicts.

Man's real history, Marx taught, is that of the different stages in the development of his systems for meeting his production requirements. This is all there is to history; there is no revelation therein of any pre-existent Divine Idea. But history's pattern remains that of "the dialectic." "For the battle of ideas Marx substitutes a battle of economic forces, waged by means of the social classes which are the product of these forces. One set of economic forces raises a particular class to power, and this class makes a State in its own image, for the enforcement of its desires upon society as a whole. But no class can rule without bringing an antagonistic class into play." * Later on we shall see how Marx developed these basic ideas into his doctrine of class war and the need for violent revolution.

Feuerbach had criticized most philosophy for being too much mere speculation; Marx found Feuerbach too much inclined merely to speculate himself. For Karl Marx was impatient with any philosophy that was not a stimulus to direct action. He wrote, "The philosophers hitherto have only interpreted the world in various ways; the thing is, however, to change it!" We of today are only too aware how well Marx succeeded in his attempt to do so.

* *Encyclopædia Britannica,* 14th Ed. Article on Karl Marx.

7

Karl Marx—History as Class War

WE HAVE dealt at length with the philosophic roots of Marxism. Now we must take a brief look at the political and economic scene in Europe at the time of the publication of *A Communist Manifesto* in 1848.

The developments following the spread of the Industrial Revolution had been exactly those which, you will remember, Thomas Jefferson had dreaded. Mass production in the new, roaring factories had ruined home industry. People from the country were forced to pour into the cities where they formed a supply of cheap labor for the factories. This kept wages at the level of mere subsistence, or lower. Thus an urban civilization marked by great disproportion of wealth was created— just what Jefferson had feared as a threat to the successful functioning of a "free society."

You cannot read of the excesses and evils of the early years of the capitalist era without wondering if the system which perpetrated them can ever justify itself. In those years there was no protection whatsoever for the workers. There were no laws to prevent the exploitation of women and children, no insurance against accident or illness, no old age support, no sanitary regulations, no unions to battle for better conditions. Men, women, and little children were flung into modern industry to work as long as they could, and then to be cast aside to die through exhaustion, or to cough out their lungs with consumption. The employer had everything his own way. He had also, in the "pleasure-value" theory developed from Hume, a philosophic ground for accumulating wealth on the basis of the belief that eventually the new system would produce the greatest happiness for the greatest number. He had, moreover, on the basis of Locke's political doctrines, a plausible ground for demanding that government should protect his "property" as its main function.

It is small wonder that the bitterness of Marx against actual living conditions, and against the philosophic background on which industrial society rested, knew no bounds. The misery which had been created, and which society tried to *excuse,* was beyond our belief. We can find out about it by reading descriptions of what life was like in the early nineteenth century in such a fast growing center of industry as Manchester, England. Nor was life very pleasant for the worker in the new industrial centers of our own land. But here there was always the margin of hope that an unexploited continent maintained.

In Europe there was no such margin—except for those who could escape to America and to the Utopia it still promised. For the toiling and oppressed masses in the new industrial towns the dream of a better life based on the foundations of a "free society" was fading fast. Political freedom which, in western Europe, had been welcomed where it was new, and treasured where it was old, began to seem an empty boon. To a work-weary father watching his ten year old child die from overwork in the mills, the lot of his ancestors as serfs on the land of their medieval lord may well have seemed desirable. Freedom from such servitude, the right to move freely about, to vote, to express his own opinion, were inadequate compensations for the conditions of the life he must face. It was time for a new dream to be born.

Before we begin to describe that dream we must emphasize one aspect of life in most European countries which still persists, and which was omnipresent in the days of Marx. This is the stratification of people into clearly defined "classes." Of course, the class concept is not unknown to us. In some of our older cities there still remains a social hierarchy based on family prestige. But such distinctions are not taken seriously by more than an insignificant number of us, and they play no great part in the life of our land. Our "aristocracy" is primarily one of wealth, and its basis is, therefore, far more fluid. There has never been among us the feeling that a poor man's son need stay poor, nor, for that matter, that a rich man's necessarily stay rich. The possession of wealth may make it possible for a few to live on the labor of many. But no one is entitled to do so because he belongs to a "class" privileged by birth or title.

Partly because of its heritage from the medieval world picture, Europe still, at least west of the "Iron Curtain," is characterized by the stratifying effect of centuries of class distinctions of which wealth is only the most recent determining factor. Family, ownership of land, titles, even if long since officially unrecognized, all play their part in maintaining distinctions of class unknown in this country. Many of us have been amused at the way in which people from Holland or Belgium, or even democratic Switzerland, will "place" an individual according to birth or special privilege. Those of us who remember the wonderful picture of early twentieth-century European society given in Jacob Wassermann's *The World's*

Illusion will recall how such distinctions characterize so recent a period.

In Great Britain, for example, distinctions still persist to a degree that seems amazing to the American visitor. You still find it hard to get the same sort of direct man-to-man contact between, let us say, the "well-born" son of an estate holder, poor as present taxes may make him, and the farmer who works his land, that you would have here in our country between similar individuals. Too many generations of class distinction get in the way of such direct, uncomplicated contact.

This is a digression, perhaps a helpful one, however. Karl Marx's social theories were based squarely upon a fierce preoccupation with the distinction between different "classes," with "class consciousness," and with the resulting social struggles. The European background of class society made this far more natural than it would have been in our relatively classless country. This factor, together with greater distress and lesser compensating hope, made it inevitable that Marxism should have been born in Europe, not in America.

Many of us have never realized how fortunate the United States has been in failing to acquire the rigid distinctions of class which have long been a bane to European society, and a barrier to peaceful social progress. To most Americans the sharp division of society into clearly defined and recognizable classes seems puzzling. We are unfamiliar with the Marxian patter about proletarians, semi-proletarians, bourgeoisie, petty-bourgeoisie, intellectuals, etc., because our own society is not so sharply divided. Because of this, all such talk seems to us to consist of dangerous and unnecessary abstraction from reality.

If we can understand the rigid class system, the economic evil, of Europe in his day, we are ready to understand Karl Marx and his influence. In the German philosophers he had at hand the theoretical elements with which to build; in the grinding poverty and disillusionment of the working classes of Europe the setting against which his Utopia was projected. Had these two sets of factors not coincided we could not have had Marxism in the form in which it developed.

Marx was born of a Jewish family in Trier, on the border between France and Germany. He studied there, went on to Berlin for more advanced work, returned to his home city, lived later in Cologne, Paris, and all his last years in London. In 1848 he published, in partnership with Friedrich Engels, *A Communist Manifesto;* later he presented the world with the monumental work, *Capital.* The second was a detailed indictment of the sort of society which had developed on the theoretic bases of Locke and Hume, and the practical foundation of the Industrial Revolution: a free, "laissez-faire" social order. The first was a battle cry, the echoes of which have never died, and which still resound in our world today. We shall examine this document in some detail. Whether we like it or not, it ranks with our own Declaration and with the New Testament as a force which has changed the life of mankind.

Friedrich Engels, who collaborated with Marx in writing the Manifesto, was the son of a wealthy manufacturer at Barmen in the Rhineland who also had factories in Manchester, England. He was brilliant, charming, talented. He enjoyed music, painting, and was a connoisseur of good wine. He was an atheist who rediscovered God in Hegel's Absolute Idea. He was almost the exact opposite of the dour, vehement, vitriolic Marx. Except in one way—they were as one in the development of the theory of communism. They did not "invent" communism; there were already many Communists. But they gave to communism a new theoretical basis—"Dialectical Materialism." On this basis, they gave communism a fixed, orthodox "line" which has been revered as a gospel ever since, and which provided the bases for the establishment of the Soviet Union. Without such a basis, communism could never have developed into such a dangerous doctrine. Its real dangers are not the economic and social reforms which it advances so much as its terrible insistence on the need for *violence* in obtaining them, and for *repression* of all opposing opinion.

The Communist Party line was set by the Manifesto of 1848. This brief, explosive document begins with the statement, "A spectre is haunting Europe—the spectre of communism." Remember, this was written more than one hundred years ago. It brings to our minds, however, a strange sense of the familiar. Our world is haunted by the same "spectre," but the form in which we now fear it is its present identification with the national power of the Soviet Union and of China.

Another familiar note struck in the opening of the Manifesto is found in the statement that all political parties brand their opponents as *communistic* when they wish to defame them. For one hundred years this charge has been made indiscriminately by conservative groups everywhere against all those who oppose them. But those who regard themselves as true Communists recognize as their real brothers only those who follow the "line" of Marx and Lenin. They detest all the more moderate socialists.

The Manifesto, the gospel from which the party line derives, continues with the assertion, "The history of all hitherto existing society is the history of class struggles." Later, it is true, Marx did hold that in very early times there had been a sort of "primitive communism" in which, since all shared alike in land and goods, there had been a "classless" social order not characterized by struggle. But that order, if indeed it ever actually existed, had vanished in the dawn mists of history. In recorded times, Marx insisted, struggle between bitterly opposed classes had been the normal social situation.

Without, for the moment, stopping to ask if this is really true, we shall go on to examine the "message" of the Manifesto, that challenge to action by the oppressed workers of the world. Then we shall show how it is grounded in those philosophic roots with which we have been dealing. Finally, we shall see how its principles became embodied in the formation of the Soviet Union by Lenin in 1917.

The Manifesto presents, as the current phase of a perennial class warfare that has marked all history, the struggle between the "bourgeoisie" and the "proletariat." The former are the employers, the exploiters, the owners of "the means of production," which, in an industrial society, are the mines, the factories, the tools, all the sinews of industry. The latter are the dispossessed and exploited workers who are, therefore, at the mercy of the bourgeoisie. The term bourgeoisie originally referred to the free citizens of a Bourg, the French equivalent of our word "borough." It was later extended to include the whole class, or the many classes, between the workers and the nobility. Gradually it became identified with that "middle class" which engaged in trade. Proletariat was used collectively for those classes of a political community who depend for their livelihood on their daily labor at wages set by others. The derivation is from a Latin word, *Proletarius,* used of those citizens who, having no property of their own, could be of use to the state only by providing it with their *proles,* that is, their children. The whole of the Communist Manifesto is a searing blast at the bourgeois class. Its argument shows how that class came into power, what its iniquities are, how it prepares the way for its own downfall, and what the proletariat must do to speed its final overthrow.

Now Marx, as you will remember, followed the lead of Feuerbach in accepting a "materialistic" approach to the understanding of society. He singled out "production relations" as being basic in supplying the key to the comprehension of any particular social group or period. Those who own the means or instruments of production constitute the ruling class, and are, therefore, opposed by all those who do not. In an agricultural society, such as had existed in the medieval period, those who owned the *land,* the feudal nobility, made up the ruling class. But the Industrial Revolution had put power into the hands of those who owned the new instruments of production, and it is this class that Marx called the bourgeoisie.

We may well ask whether it is really true that *all* society is *always* so sharply divided into such warring classes, and whether it is natural for all men to have such a fierce "class consciousness" as Marxist theory requires. We shall return to this question later. Of the bourgeoisie, Marx says, "An oppressed class under the sway of the feudal nobility, an armed and self-governing association in the medieval commune, cornerstone of the great monarchies in general, the bourgeoisie has at last, since the establishment of Modern Industry and of the world market, conquered for itself, in the modern representative state, exclusive political sway."

It is very illuminating to note that Marx attributed to the bourgeoisie not only an exaggerated continuity and solidarity, but also a sort of secret, "cabalistic" organization. He implies that there had been a sort of bourgeois plot to seize power, which had been put into effect as a result of a conscious plan, at the moment when modern industry had sufficiently changed the nature of society to make this possible. He attributes to the bourgeoisie the sort of revolutionary organization, and the sort of revolutionary "coup," that he is urging the proletariat to organize, and bring off.

Now this just had not been true. There had, of course, been a large number of those whom Marx would class as bourgeoisie among those who were leaders in the British, American, and French revolutions—which had prepared the way for the "rule of the bourgeoisie." But there had not been, in any of these historic overturnings, an exclusive, organized role played by such a "class." In seventeenth-century England the motive for revolution was primarily religious. In our own revolution, land owners, tradesmen, poor farmers, workers, and "intellectuals" had all rallied to the standards of a nation based on the concepts of personal liberty as outlined by Locke. In France, the "masses" had certainly played their part along with any element that might have been classed as bourgeois. Any unbiased view sees the revolutions of the late eighteenth century as based *primarily* on man's passionate desire for more of personal freedom and political equality based on philosophic foundations by now familiar to us. To see them as the result primarily of a bourgeois plot is certainly a distortion.

This may not seem of major importance to our present inquiry. But it is significant, nevertheless, because it questions the validity of Marx's insistence that all social change is the result of the struggle between classes, organized as such and conscious of their distinctive common interests. This, to a less "indoctrinated" point of view, may well seem a dangerous half truth. Such common interests do exist, as does common consciousness of them, and a degree, sometimes highly developed, of organization to protect them. But to interpret all history in such terms is a shocking oversimplification.

It may well be that the fierce and dogmatic hold which Marxist principles have had for so many is due largely to this oversimplification of the forces at play in social problems. It is so much easier to interpret these problems, and to suggest solutions for them, if you reduce them to only one set of factors. Those who have followed Marx have insisted that the *only* factors of importance are those having to do with "production relations." You can forget about all man's hopes, fears, and beliefs, reducing them to their bearing on his economic situation. This makes it ever so much easier to prescribe an ideal society, and to feel that you are being "scientific" in your prescription. Then, if you add to this so-called scientific approach a burning sense of the wrongs suffered by an underprivileged class, you have the two main motivating factors of the powerful appeal of Marxism.

We shall find, however, that Marx's account of the way in which our industrial sort of society develops, once it has begun, is hard to refute. As to the inferences for action which he draws from his account—well, that is another matter.

The account in the Manifesto of the pattern for the development of control by the bourgeoisie, and of its inevitable decline, is classic and still definitive for the Marxian school of thought. The bourgeoisie gains power because it owns the "instruments of production," which are, as we said, the mines, the factories, the tools. This power, once acquired by a class, will never be surrendered voluntarily. The only way that such power can be broken by those who are opposed to the class which holds it is by a violent revolution in which the instruments of production are seized. Since the bourgeoisie controls the State wherever it holds sway, and uses the State to perpetuate its power, the dispossessed class, the proletariat, must overturn and get control of the State in order to seize the instruments of production.

The Manifesto continues with an account of why such an overturn will become not only desirable, but inevitable as well. The bourgeoisie is self-condemned to destruction because it constantly narrows the number of those who belong to it. By ceaseless improvement in the means and methods of production, it constantly diminishes the opportunities for employment, and creates a larger and larger "reserve army" of laborers who are unemployed. Also, by bigger and bigger business combinations, it cuts down its strength by reducing the number of those who have a stake in the continuance of its power. This last is a sound comment on the grave danger to capitalism inherent in its tendency towards monopoly.

Thus the ranks of the proletariat are constantly being swollen, while those of the bourgeoisie are being diminished. Moreover, the insecurity, distress, and resentment of the proletariat increase steadily as there is less and less for the many and more and more for the few. Marx held that redress of the grievances of the oppressed was impossible through peaceful means; harmonizing their interests with those of the diminished, frightened, and powerful bourgeoisie is out of the question. Therefore, sooner or later, at the proper time, under the leadership of those who best understand their interests, the proletariat will revolt. By *violent means* they will overturn the State, and thus be able to seize the "instruments of production."

Thus far there has been a straight and compelling logic about the argument of the Manifesto—if you accept the premises on which it is based. But the proletarian revolution does not merely supplant one class which has held power by another, as all other revolutions have done. It creates a "classless" society, one in which everyone is a proletarian, and in which the age-old class struggle comes to an end. All private property is done away with, and, since the State exists to protect such property, all need for political organization will gradually cease. The Manifesto ends with the well known words, "The Communists disdain to conceal their views and aims. They openly declare that their ends can be attained only by the forcible overthrow of all existing social conditions. Let the ruling classes tremble at a Communist revolution. The proletarians have nothing to lose but their chains. They have a world to win. Working men of all countries, unite!"

Thus Marx did forecast another and *final* revolution. There was to be no more need for revolutionary activity; a true social Utopia, though he hated that word, was to be attained. The Soviet Union of today was founded squarely on the application of his principles. As our motto is *E Pluribus Unum,* so might theirs be *Ne Plus Ultra.* Indeed, Andrei Vishinsky says in *The Law of the Soviet State,* "The Soviet state represents the expression of the highest possible form of democracy."

We can stop only briefly to criticize the doctrine of the Communist Manifesto before returning to its philosophic roots, to expose which is our primary purpose. But there are certain comments that we must make. In the first place, the history of the last hundred years has proved that "the workers," call them the proletariat if you wish to keep Marx's terminology, have been able to win for themselves a vast improvement in living conditions in many lands without revolution. Developments in our country bear this out. Consider, for one concrete example, the shamefully slow but gradually succeeding drive for adequate "child-labor" laws. Bitterly fought at first as an "infringement of free enterprise," they have gradually extended at least partial protection against the employment of children. Or consider the development of "social security" programs, free clinics, etc. Not for one moment should we feel that such steps as have been taken are sufficient; the fight for improved labor conditions goes on, and must do so. But the organization of labor has given to it a degree of power that Marx did not believe possible under "bourgeois" control. It has brought on the scene in recent years in our own country labor leaders whose power rivals that of the leaders of industry. The idea that "the workers" were in for a worse and worse fate in capitalist society has not been proved true. The very word, "proletarian," is either unknown to most "workers" in this country, or is used jokingly if at all.

On the other hand, the dangerous tendency towards monopoly, towards bigger and bigger business combinations, has developed in some ways very much as Marx predicted. Capitalism, to be a healthy and workable system, must keep opportunities open for small business, opportunities which in many fields have already ceased to exist. Holding companies, chain-stores, radio networks, and newspaper syndicates are all examples of this trend. Free Enterprise, in the opinion of many, is threatened far more by this overdevelopment of its own monopolistic tendencies than by the menace of communism.

We must not dwell on these social and economic considerations. But there is one comment on the Manifesto, more political in its nature, that should be briefly made at this point. Why did Marx assume, naively it seems to us, that a proletarian revolution would bring about a classless society, and end the perennial class struggle? He apparently had confidence that when the "expropriators," the bourgeoisie, had been "expropriated" by the proletariat, the latter would all share in managing civil affairs so that, as Engels was to say, "the mechanism of the state" could "wither away." He did not foresee that after *any* violent revolution power will pass into the hands of some group smaller than the populace as a whole.

It is certainly a far cry from Jefferson's ideas as to the nature of the state to those of Marx. With his different, Lockean background, Jefferson took it as evident that the state should be a voluntary association of *all* those who agreed to its organization. Its purpose was to make the liberty and property of all more secure. But Marx, with his background of Fichte and Hegel, thinks of the state as an agent of the *will*. He goes further and disconnects the state from society as a whole. To him, the state is a more restricted organization *within* society, and its purpose is to make more effective the control of society by those who, through their ownership of the means of production, dominate it. Lenin was to say later, "According to Marx, the state is an organ of class *domination*, an organ of oppression of one class by another; its aim is the creation of 'order' which legalizes and perpetuates this oppression." This it does by having "special bodies of armed men which have prison at their disposal," and "the right to collect taxes."

Lenin did admit that there were different degrees to which this might be true. Fascism was a particularly virulent form of the repressive state—a "democratic-bourgeois" form was preferable, for, "without parliamentarianism, without the elective right, the development of the working class would be impossible." Yet he still found it necessary to characterize "every type of bourgeois state—even the most 'democratic'— as a machine to crush and repress the toilers, as a bludgeon in the hands of the exploiters as against the exploited."

Only through examining the roots of Marxism-Leninism can we come to understand fully why such a view of the state, distorted and perverted as it seems to us, is natural to the disciples of Marx.

Let's go back to the statement, "The history of all hitherto existing society is the history of class struggles," and note how easily, indeed, how inevitably, Marx had come to this view. Granted, he was agonizingly aware of the struggle between employers and workers in the new, raw, industrial society in which he lived. Obviously, he was passionately espousing the workers' cause in that struggle. Their cause cried out to him in the streets of the Rhenish industrial towns, as it had to Engels in the slums of Manchester. There was no doubt that a fierce class antagonism was the outstanding characteristic of European society at the time. But what, for Marx, elevated that current conflict into the chief attribute of history involved other factors than the mere observation of conditions as they were. It involved elements from his philosophic background, which was permeated by the thinking of Fichte and Hegel.

Fichte had flooded the German mind with the idea of the self as a center of the will, and had characterized its essential activity as struggle, and the overcoming of opposition. Because of this philosophic element in his thinking, Marx found it easy to generalize the current conflict in industrial society into an historic principle characterizing all society. The "class" is a more inclusive and more effective focus for the expression of will, and for carrying on struggle, than is any mere individual.

From Fitchte, Marx derived this doctrine of struggle as basic in all society. Of course, elements of tension based on conflicting interests can be found within almost any human group. To study these is more than legitimate. But to make them the *sole* touchstone for understanding such groups is a vast distortion, one impossible for any theorist not permeated with the Fichtean background.

From Hegel, Marx took the doctrine of the "dialectical" movement of all history. Atheist as he was, intolerant of Hegel's Absolute Idea, avowed foe of all that was occult and mystic, Marx still regarded the dialectical principle with a reverence that matched that of a religious zealot for Divine

Revelation. He held that the modern, industrial society in which he lived represented one step in a particular manifestation of the dialectical process, one that had yet to complete itself. We must take account of his doctrine.

In that doctrine, we should consider first feudal society, with its Aristotelian background, with its graded social order, its lords and ladies, its serfs and bonded servants. Here you have a "thesis," not one "revealed" by any Divine Idea, but one developing naturally from the "production relations" of the time, in which the land-owning class and the agricultural workers represented the two sides of the social struggle. This thesis asserted the rule of the nobility, the owners of the *land,* the current "means of production." But, as in all cases, the rule of any one class brings an antagonistic class into play; this presents an antithesis. Thus the "bourgeoisie," the class between the nobility and the workers, became organized, and, as society became industrialized, by gaining control of the new means of production, mines, factories, etc., seized all power and set up the sort of state which would perpetuate its control.

Now the world awaits another revolution, a synthesis of the first two stages. And this can be nothing but the proletarian revolution, by means of which the exploited toilers will seize the instruments of production, smash the bourgeois state, and set up their own, "classless" society.

Note that this *must* occur. Here is where Marx's mystical belief in the constant operation of the dialectical process comes in. It is strange, in a way, that he held such a fanatical conviction about it, and it proves the hold that the Hegelian world picture had upon him. For Marx insisted that his thinking was completely naturalistic. It was not, of course. Later, we shall criticize the foundations on which it rested. But Marx always insisted that the dialectic was the key to comprehension of history, and his devoted followers still regard it as basic.

Now this explains something very essential in the doctrine of the true Marxist; it explains why he must *insist* upon revolu-

tion, upon change by violent means. This insistence is not
based upon bloodthirstiness. It is not based on a desire to
avenge the real sufferings of the proletariat. It is based upon
the deep conviction that until the *second revolution,* that of
the proletariat, occurs, a great historic process is in suspense,
and a cycle of the historic dialectic process has failed to
complete itself. The bourgeois revolution which promised
political freedom brought the "antithesis" to the old "thesis"
of the medieval world. Now all the world is waiting for the
"synthesis." That is why the proletarian revolution *must* occur,
occur as a matter not of social justice but of "historic necessity."
The true Marxist awaits this completion with that sort of
impatience, both logical and emotional, with which the musician awaits the final chord which will resolve all the preceding
disharmony.

There is another element in the thinking of Karl Marx which
came straight out of his Hegelian heritage. That is the trouble-
some concept that "the real is the rational," which, you will
remember, we dealt with before. It holds that what happens in
history happens because it is *right,* no matter how hard it is
to accept it as such. For Hegel, believing as he did that the
entire history of the world was the making actual of what the
Absolute Idea intended, the concept was logical. For Marx,
who claimed to have exorcised the Divine in any form from
his thinking, it was not so logically grounded. Nevertheless,
he clung to it as he did to that other Hegelian doctrine, the
dialectic. It gave to him and to his disciples the conviction
that what the "dialectic process" of social history must bring to
pass—the proletarian revolution—would be *right* in the same
sense as Hegel's unfolding in history of the designs of the
Absolute Idea.

These, then, are the main elements in Marx's philosophic
background to keep in mind in studying his system and Soviet
Russia, the political embodiment thereof. The essence of the
human being, of the self, is the exercise of *will* and the over-

coming of opposition. The state, or, with Marx, the *class*, is a better focus for such activity than the individual, and therefore the individual should submit his will to that of the larger unit. Only thus can the working class, the proletariat, speed its coming to power. In doing so, it must accept the leadership of orthodox, Marxian Communism, which must be organized by an omnipotent Party system to which unquestioning obedience must be given. Marx had no liking for the State, but, as in so many other ways, he disagreed with Hegel and yet followed the Hegelian pattern of thought by transferring Hegel's attitude toward the State to the Party. Always he insisted that history, the record of class struggles, proceeds according to the pattern of the dialectic, and that what this pattern brings to pass must be *right* because of "historic necessity."

We shall find, as we complete our inquiry with a study of how these concepts went into the formation of the Soviet Union, that it is these very elements which are dangerous to the world. For they explain the "closed mind" that marks the Marxist disciples who plan Soviet policies.

In the development of his basic theories Marx accomplished much of permanent importance to his fellow men. He overthrew the "pleasure theory of value" and established instead what is called the "labor theory." This holds that the worth of any article is determined by the amount and kind of toil that goes into its making. Thus the most important element in "production relations" is the human element, the men and women engaged in producing the commodities which the world needs. From this recognition has come almost all the progress made towards safeguarding "human rights" in our industrial society. The need for further progress in this field offers a healthy challenge to our own traditional concept that the state is concerned primarily with protecting "property rights" rather than "human rights." No capitalist society can exist today that does not make some compromises where these two types of rights conflict.

We can readily admit the necessity for accepting some measures that are "socialist" in character, and our country has accepted many, and will have to accept more. But that does not mean that we should not guard against acceptance of the Communist Party "line," which still is based squarely upon that dangerous philosophic background which we have discussed.

It was an historic tragedy of the first magnitude that Marx's message to the world combined, in its impassioned appeal, so much that was needed in the way of social reform with so much that was poisoned with this dangerous philosophic background. There was so much that was good in the package of his thought, had it not been tied up with the strings of a type of philosophy already tending towards totalitarianism. We have discussed the foreboding factors in that philosophy in general terms. The best way to bring out their concrete effects is to turn our attention to the Soviet Union, that political embodiment of the ideas of Marx and Engels as applied by Lenin and Stalin, and as now interpreted by Khrushchev.

8

The Soviet Union—
The State as the Will to
Power

EUROPE in the middle of the nineteenth century sorely needed a new vision to sustain the imaginations and fire the hopes of its disillusioned millions. The warm, bright glow cast upon the world by the preceding great dream, that of political freedom, was fast fading, though less than a century had passed since it had found expression in the United States. There, in the presence of unparalleled opportunities, its magic persisted. But the toiling masses of Europe's new "wage-slaves" found little comfort in it. Even where political freedom had been won, the right to vote carried no assurance of decent employment or, indeed, enough to eat. In many parts of Europe, especially in all of eastern areas, there had not even been a "bourgeois" revolution, and conditions remained essentially feudal until recently.

But it was not in the east of Europe, certainly not in Russia, that Marx and Engels expected the "proletariat" to rise in arms. Russia was by far the most backward of the great powers of Europe in any kind of social reform, and represented to the authors of the Manifesto a stronghold of despotism destined to stand in the path of progress. Indeed, Engels studied Russian merely because he thought that either he or Marx should know "the languages, the history, the literature, and the details of the social institutions of those nations with which, precisely, we shall immediately be coming into conflict."

As a matter of fact, it was in Germany that Marx expected the proletarian revolution to occur first. At that time, the German states, not yet united into a single nation, had, for the most part, not had even a bourgeois revolution. Marx and Engels held that such a step was first necessary, from a theoretic, "dialectical" point of view, to provide an "antithesis" to feudal society; from a practical point of view to create the industrialized conditions under which alone the proletariat could rise. Thus, in the closing paragraphs, their Manifesto states, "The Communists turn their attention chiefly to Germany, because that country is on the eve of a bourgeois revolution, that is bound to be carried out under more advanced conditions of European civilization, and with a more developed proletariat, than that of England was in the seventeenth and of France in the eighteenth century, and because the bourgeois revolution in Germany will be but the prelude to an immediately following proletarian revolution."

In 1848, the very year of the Manifesto, revolution broke out in many parts of Germany, as well as in France. There, the "Paris Commune" for a time seemed to offer an opportunity for the embodiment of Marx's principles. But it did not endure, and in Germany revolutionary activity was abortive. It resulted in a certain amount of social reforms by the government, and in driving most of the revolutionaries, largely "bourgeois" in character, to the United States.

During the rest of the nineteenth century, the development of world trade, the opening of new markets, and the demand for commodities of all kinds brought an increasing measure of prosperity to much of Europe and rendered living conditions slightly more tolerable. Marx died in 1883, Engels in 1895, and still there was no sign of an immediate proletarian revolution anywhere. The Communists were becoming divided; some believed in compromising with existing "bourgeois" governments and trying to obtain better working conditions by peaceful means. The others, the true disciples, put "doctrine" above expediency and persisted in calling for revolution by violence, for seizure of the state and the means of production by the armed proletariat. At the 1903 Congress of the Communists in Brussels, this division became a definite split between the Mensheviks, the minority who were willing to compromise, and the Bolsheviks, the majority who insisted upon revolution. Note that the latter clung to the belief that this was *necessary* in the old sense that the dialectical process must fulfill itself.

If there was gradual progress towards the recognition of "human rights" in many parts of Europe, there was certainly none in Czarist Russia. As late as 1905, hundreds of men and and women peaceably demonstrating in front of the palace in St. Petersburg were shot down by orders of the Czar. Later the same year revolts of workers in Moscow, and of sailors at Sevastapol, were put down with inconceivable savagery. Famine, ignorance, and superstition made the life of the poor masses in Russia unbearable.

It was not until the first World War, however, that the groaning distress of the Russian people precipitated revolt. The additional privations resulting from war, and the spreading knowledge of corruption in the government, conspired to bring about the revolution which forced the Czar to abdicate, and which put in power the "bourgeois" government headed by Kerensky early in the year 1917.

Meanwhile, and for many years, the Bolshevik wing of the Communist Party had been led by the Russian, Lenin, born Vladimir Ulyanov, at Simbirsk on the Volga. The name by which the world knows him he assumed as a sort of "party name" when he gave up all other interests to work for the Marxist cause of revolution. Through all the disagreements and divisions of the Communists, Lenin championed the absolute following of the doctrines of Marx and Engels. His devotion to such doctrine can be likened only to that of a Disciple for the True Faith. He vehemently attacked all ideas of compromise with the bourgeoisie as "opportunism" and furiously denounced all those who accepted this "Menshevik" attitude as "traitors."

But even Lenin had not expected that developments would occur in Russia which would set the stage for the proletarian revolution of which he dreamed and for which he lived. When he was informed of the Kerensky revolt in March of 1917 he was living with his wife in Zurich, and heard only indirectly of the developments in his own land. Immediately he sought some way of reaching Russia, and this desire was facilitated by the German government. They knew Lenin would urge his countrymen to make peace on terms favorable to Germany. They did not foresee how successful he would be in other ways.

In April, 1917, Lenin arrived in Petrograd, which had been St. Petersburg, and was later to bear his own name. He came to a vast, poor, backward nation, bled white by war, a nation still reeling from the long delayed bourgeois uprising which had finally overturned that medieval relict, the regime of the Czar. Six short months later, by his superb leadership, his utter devotion to Marx's teachings, and his iron determination to apply them to the letter in reforming his nation, he had brought about a true proletarian revolution for the first time in history and had set up the Soviet State.

Whatever we may think of its ultimate results, few incidents in history are more dramatic than Lenin's arrival at the Finland Station in Petrograd late at night on April 16, 1917. As Edmund Wilson tells us, when Lenin emerged from the train he did not hesitate a moment. Speaking first at the station, then at the palace which had already become the headquarters of the Communist Party, he stunned his hearers by insisting that there must be a second, proletarian revolution. To accomplish this, the war with Germany must be ended at once; the bourgeois, Kerensky government must be turned out of office; local Soviets, councils of peasants and workers, similar to one already existing among the workers of Petrograd, must be set up all over the land. Most important of all, the peasants, soldiers, sailors, and workers must take power into their own hands. Only by overthrowing the Kerensky government could they "remove the bureaucrats from office," and seize the "means of production."

History has never seen a more exact application of theory to practice than occurred when Lenin organized the Soviet Union. Whatever changes have developed later in the literal observance of Marxist principles by the Soviet government, its original idea and impetus came straight out of Marx. But we must also consider other factors in the Russian heritage which made that country so unexpectedly suited to sustain such a form of government.

We have referred to the appalling conditions under which the vast majority of the Russians had lived. Moreover, industrialization had begun so late in Russia that there had not been time for any progress towards decent standards of life for industrial workers under the leadership of labor organization and collective bargaining. Nor would such progress have developed easily, if at all, under such a reactionary regime. Therefore, the feeling that tolerable conditions could be achieved only through violence was already widespread. Then, too, there had never been in Russia a sufficiently numerous propertied "class," or a sufficient number of educated people, to provide a basis for political democracy as we know it. Those two essential foundations of the spirit of freedom, specified by Locke, and prized by Jefferson, were almost completely lacking.

Not only had there been merciless oppression of the people under the rule of the Romanoffs; there had also been in common usage those very same methods of control by espionage, anonymous report, and tests of political loyalty which the Soviet regime has relied upon and perfected. Russia was a "police state" long before she became a Communist one. Perhaps we do not need to look further for reasons to explain the amazing passivity of the Russian people towards rigid control of their lives by the government in power. At least under the Soviet system they have the feeling, be it real or illusory, that they are themselves the source of such power of control.

Another influence which has long conditioned the Russians to the unquestioning acceptance of authority has been that of the Orthodox Church. This had been their source of spiritual comfort, and of aesthetic satisfaction as well, for many centuries. The philosophic tap-roots of the Orthodox Church had been somewhat the same as those of the Church of Rome. But the far closer contact of the Orthodox Church with the mystical approach of the Orient to religion had diminished the importance of any rational grounds for faith. On the other hand, it had increased the emphasis on mysticism and passion —as evidenced in the elaborately beautiful rituals of the Russian Church. It seems very probable that a people so swiftly deprived of their accustomed outlet for aesthetic and religious feeling as were the Russians after 1917, through the suppression of the Church, would naturally transfer their needs for such an outlet to such a dynamic political "faith" as Marxism— especially since the creed of Marx is one that requires struggle and sacrifice from its devoted followers.

Our speculations about these contributory influences to the

success of Marxism in Russia may or may not be valid. In any case, they were very minor streams of influence compared to the furious spate of Lenin's fanatical resolve to create in Russia, on the spur of the opportunity suddenly offered, a proletarian socialist state on the Marxian model.

Marx, with his view of the state as a device for oppression of all "classes" except the one in power, saw little need for such organization in a "classless" society. Therefore, he made very few suggestions as to what political forms would be necessary after the success of the proletarian revolution. When the proletariat has overturned the existing state, taken control of the means of production from the bourgeoisie, and made them all public instead of private property, there would be no need for a state system designed to protect special interests. The next step was to be "the withering away of the State," as Engels described it. He and Marx had rather naively believed that, in a classless society, ordinary citizens could carry on whatever public work might be necessary without being in any way differentiated from their fellows. All special privileges and immunities, higher standards of pay, uniforms of office, etc., were to be done away with. Speaking of carrying on the affairs of government, Lenin said, "it will be possible to perform them for 'workingmen's wages,' which circumstance can and must strip those functions of every shadow of privilege, of every appearance of official grandeur." How surprised some of the earlier Marxists would be at the exalted position of government officials in the Russia of today.

Karl Marx always railed against Utopian schemers, always prided himself on being realistic, clear, "down to earth." Yet he seems to have had the mystic belief that the proletarian revolution would so change human nature as to make such a dream world possible. Somehow, the rank and file of the people, unused as they were to managing their own affairs, were to discover within themselves the ability to carry on all the work of the state without any long and arduous courses of special training.

Of course, Marx and Engels did point out that all these developments could not occur at once. For some time after the proletarian revolution it would be necessary to maintain the "dictatorship of the proletariat" in order to fight "reaction and counter-revolution." Those dangers would remain until all the bourgeoisie were liquidated, until all accepted the principles of Marx, until all possible effective centers of opposition were removed. Then and then only could one find real "democracy." Later, even democracy, which is still a "form of the state," would itself "wither away."

The first thing to note here is that your true Marxist believes that democracy can be found only in a "classless society," the sort which is to follow the proletarian revolution after it has overcome all vestiges of opposition. He is taught to believe that under capitalism there is no true democracy because various special interests, especially "big business," wield the real power, and government "by the people" is only a mockery. Elections, for example, are always controlled by the big business interests, and the people have only the illusion that they are running the affairs of their nation. We ourselves are sure this is no longer true. Indeed, only a Marxist completely blinded by dogma could claim that the election of 1945 in England, or that of 1948 in the United States, was controlled and managed by "big business." But the danger does still exist.

The Marxist believes that it is perfectly logical—at least for the purposes of propaganda—to call a government "democratic" even though it is run entirely by the Communist Party. In the Soviet Union, and in the countries it dominates, there is only one political party, only one list of candidates at elections, a list prepared by the party from which the voters may choose. No organized opposition of any kind is permitted, nor is any other point of view allowed to appear in print or to be heard on the air. The only discussion possible is that which deals with the relative merits of candidates or of plans for furthering the designs of the Party. But still this is the really "democratic" way of doing things because thus only can the "working people" be protected from the "control" of reactionary, "bourgeois" influences. Otherwise such interests might interfere with the plans of the Party for the further socialist development of the state for the benefit of the people.

This peculiar, and to us distorted, concept of "democracy" explains how it is possible for Russia to claim that a government in one of her satellite states is "democratic" even though it has been put into power by the shameless use of pressure, and has supervised elections in which only the Communist Party supplies the candidates. It is democratic because it has liquidated all those "special interests" which, in the Marxist view, make democracy only a travesty in capitalist lands. Yet to us it seems outrageous to call such a government democratic. We know well that such "special interests" as organized business, labor, the church, and the farm lobby do play a disproportionate part in the way of influencing our elections, and determining legislation and even foreign policy. But no one organized group in any western land wields a power today that can be compared to that held absolutely by the Communist Party in the lands under Soviet domination. By definition, "democracy" means, of course, rule by the people. Most of us are convinced that, in terms of the true meaning of the word, we enjoy a far greater measure of its realization than do those under the domination of the Soviet Union. Surely, we are often shocked by the use of undue influence by various groups in this country. But the remedy seems to most of us to lie in the direction of working to diminish their influence rather than to exchange our situation for one in which there is one all-compelling influence, that of one political party in league with military power.

Now we must turn back to the concept that, once a classless society is firmly established, the state will "wither away." This may seem a strange conclusion to the whole Marxian doctrine. Marx started out with such forceful definiteness— class war, the proletarian revolution, seizure of the means of production, making these public instead of private property, temporary dictatorship of the proletariat. And then the further course of action, instead of being clearly planned, trails off into the mists of indefiniteness. The state withers away. All right, what then? Marx gave no answer. Perhaps he logically and emotionally could not do so. The dialectic process of history—which is that of class struggle—was to come to an end with the proletarian revolution and the establishment of a classless society. Thus there was no logical reason for conceiving of any further developments. Marx so hated the idea of the state as the "means of oppression" that he was emotionally opposed to outlining any future forms which it might assume. Society could function better without any state organization—or, at least, so he thought.

Lenin worked out the establishment of the Soviet Union according to the theories of Marx and Engels. The revolution was accomplished, foreign intervention by capitalism was thwarted, and opposition at home partially liquidated by the time Lenin died in 1924. The affairs of state were in the hands of a "dictatorship." But it was not one of the proletariat; it was one of the Party. Since then things have not worked out as Marx and Engels would somewhat naively have expected. There has certainly been no withering away of the state! The Communist Party maintains a "police state" second to none in history in the ruthless suppression of all opposition. Moscow has been the seat of its worldwide activities. It makes use of nationalistic sentiment, Pan-Slavism, and, above all, the might of the Red Army to impose its will and its doctrine upon the people of the Soviet Union, and of any other lands it can dominate.

In all fairness we should point out that things might have

developed differently. They might have done so if the original vision of Marx and Engels had been realized. Remember the closing words of their Manifesto—"Working men of *all countries*—unite!" They conceived of the proletarian revolution as an international uprising which, once started in one country, would soon spread to all. Lenin, and Stalin, his heir, did find it necessary to make the maximum use of the national power of the Russian state because the revolution did *not* spread, and because Marxism has *not* become the gospel of the working men of all countries.

The historic split between Stalin and Trotsky was over the issue as to whether a true socialist state could be established and maintained in a world largely capitalist. Stalin, speaking of this question said, "There exist both dogmatic Marxism and creative Marxism. I stand on the ground of creative Marxism. And the most important principle . . . is the doctrine of the possibility of socialism being victorious in one country taken separately."

We should remember when Stalin spoke of *socialism* that Marxists do not consider the present Soviet state as completely Communist. Stalin himself once said of his country, "it has realized what the Marxists call the first or lower phase of communism." As yet its working principle can be only that of socialism, "From each according to his capacity, to each according to his toil." When the higher phase of communism can be achieved, this will be changed to "From each according to his capacity, to each according to his *needs*."

The accomplishment of this higher phase is not possible in a largely capitalistic, and thus "hostile," world because under such conditions a large part of production must go into military supplies, and thus the abundance required for full-scale communism cannot be attained. Also, in such a period, there can be no "withering away" of the state. The state remains as a machine for crushing opposition. But the new, "proletarian" state is different because it is used by a majority to crush the remains of the "exploiter minority." Thus, in this transitional period, the proletariat needs the state. But Lenin himself, in developing such a theory, distinguished between the "vanguard of the proletariat" and the remaining masses of the toilers. Thus the way was opened, on "doctrinal" grounds, for this "vanguard," made up of Party leaders, to become a new *special class,* and to use the new state to perpetuate its control.

That, most impartial observers would agree, is what has happened in the Soviet Union. But we should be prepared to admit that there may be many among Russia's present leaders who sincerely believe this is necessary in a world divided between their system and what remains of the capitalistic world. In such a world their constant fear is that of "capitalist encirclement." This fear, together with the duty of protecting Russia as the citadel of communism, they can use to increase the blind obedience of their people to their rule, and to overcome the resistance, in countries subject to their control, of all political and religious groups that may oppose it.

Now we must return to the heart of our inquiry, the philosophic roots from which grew the Marxian doctrines on which Soviet Russia was founded. We shall do so by way of a brief examination of the "Stalin Constitution" of 1936, especially with regard to its section on the Rights and Duties of Citizens. For it is in this section that the underlying philosophic concepts are most clearly exhibited.

We note at once that the rights first treated are what we call economic or social rights. The very first paragraph of the section says, "Citizens of the U.S.S.R. have the right to work, that is, are guaranteed the right to employment and payment for their work in accordance with the quality and quantity." Here we should immediately note two things. First, the significance of putting economic rights first; second, the obvious relation of this particular provision to some of the philosophic roots we have been examining.

The Marxian dream of a better world was born on a wave of disillusion with the ability of "political" rights to provide such a world. Out of economic distress came a natural emphasis on greater economic opportunity and security. Thus, in a constitution based on Marxian doctrine, first place must be given to guarantees of such opportunity and security. Just so, our own Constitution is permeated with safeguards of our political rights, to secure which our nation was founded.

Also, let us compare the section of the Soviet Constitution referred to above with Fichte's comment on the nature of the state. For it was he who had said "the state has to make provision that everyone may be able to live by his work." Thus, in the Soviet document, we find a derivation from Fichte as direct as any in our own from John Locke.

The Soviet Constitution goes on to guarantee the right to leisure and rest, to old age and sickness insurance, to education. Certainly no one can any longer object to the extension of such protection by a state to its citizens. But there is a difference in emphasis that must be underlined again. The Soviet Union is founded on a way of thinking that holds that man's best guarantee of a good life is that which protects his "economic rights"; our nation rests on a way of thinking that holds the best guarantee of a good life to be one that protects man's "political rights." This is why, in the second World War, in fighting for the "Four Freedoms," we found the first two, Freedom of Religion and of Speech, the ones that sprang first and naturally to our minds. Whereas, one may assume that the last two, Freedom from Want and from Fear, played a similar role of first importance for the Russians.

The Soviet Constitution of 1936 does turn to the guarantee of the political rights of its citizens. But note carefully its language in doing so, "In conformity with the interests of the working people, and in order to strengthen the socialist system, the citizens of the U.S.S.R. are guaranteed by law: freedom of speech; freedom of the press; freedom of assembly." Obviously, these rights, which seem to us so fundamental, and so "unalienable," are here made contingent, that is, dependent upon the interests of the working people and the development of the socialist system. The Communist Party decides to what extent they may be enjoyed, and when and how they shall be limited.

Vishinsky, in his embittered book, says, "In our state, naturally, there is and can be no place for freedom of speech, press, and so on for the foes of socialism. Every sort of attempt on their part to utilize to the detriment of the state . . . these freedoms granted to the toilers must be classified as a counter-revolutionary crime."

Again, let us remember that Fichte conceived of the rights of citizens as held only in order that they might better perform their duties. Here is a philosophic basis for the idea that such rights are contingent, and, therefore, that the state has the right to limit them.

The Soviet Constitution goes on to insure the right of the people to unite in organizations of various kinds but again "in conformity with the interests of the working people." Particularly important is the statement in the same article that "the most active and politically most conscious citizens in the ranks of the working classes" may "unite in the Communist Party of the Soviet Union." Here is the legal ground for the self-perpetuating power of the Party in Russia. Those who the party decides are the most active, and the most politically conscious, which means, of course, most indoctrinated with Marxist ideas, are the only ones permitted to swell the ranks of the party.

It is natural for us to ask why no other political parties exist in the Soviet state. With regard to this Stalin has said, "The position of our Party as the sole legal Party in the country— the monopoly of the Communist Party—is not artificial. Our Party's monopoly grew from life . . . as a result of the fact that the Social Revolutionary and Menshevik Parties went bankrupt and passed from the scene, whereas we were actively operating." This is certainly a smooth statement to cover the ruthless "liquidation" of all opposing parties! Now, Vishinsky points out, "The Soviet state . . . naturally does not include freedom of political parties . . . inasmuch as this freedom, in the conditions prevailing in the U.S.S.R., where the toilers have complete faith in the Communist Party, is necessary only for the agents of fascism and foreign reconnaissance."

In other words, it is inconceivable that any point of view except that of the Communist Party should be expressed because it would be, by definition, opposed to the interests of "the toilers."

The 1936 Constitution guarantees the right to education, and with regard to religion says, "Freedom of religious worship and freedom of anti-religious propaganda is recognized for all citizens."

We should note, however, that freedom of *religious* propaganda is not granted. Again, no doubt, because it would necessarily be against the best interests of the toilers. Here is one of the instances, which we shall later consider, of the failure of the Soviet state to realize that men have other than economic interests.

We should end our brief treatment of the form of government in Soviet Russia by returning to philosophic roots of that form. In the Soviet state are embodied the basic concepts of the nature of man, of his proper function, and of his relation to the state which Marx derived from Fichte and Hegel. It is these elements which, given political embodiment in the Soviet Union, make that nation a danger to the world.

Thus in the Soviet Union of today you will find a philosophic heritage which explains much of its behavior and much of its menace. The Soviet state, as the instrument of the Communist Party, has a ground for its aggressiveness in the concept of the nature of man as a center of will, and of his function as its expression. It has this ground because the state, as the instrument of the Party, is a better focus for such expression than are the individuals who comprise it. They, therefore, owe it their unquestioning loyalty and blind obedience. Among them, only those who are especially *active,* that is, especially good expressors of *will,* are selected to carry on the designs of the party.

Opposition in Soviet Russia is a *crime.* It is not to be permitted because "historic necessity" demands the triumph of the Marxian point of view, and nothing may stand in the path of its Juggernaut. The only Freedom is to identify your will with that of the Soviet state, the only Democracy to accept the championship by the Communist Party of the "working people," and its protection against the special interests of capitalism which are opposed to their welfare.

To further the triumph of Marxism, to prepare the way for violent revolutions of the proletariat, and the consequent establishment of a classless society, any means may be used, any lie excused, any treachery justified. For the realization of the Marxian dream is more important by far than personal integrity or present privation. It has a sanction to which is denied the character of the Divine, but which admits no less a compulsion, and is based on no less a necessity.

The loyal citizen of the Soviet state will, therefore, accept the decisions of the leaders of the Communist Party as unquestionable. He will not presume to oppose his own opinions to them. If those opinions differ, he must be "in error" because the Party *must* be right. There is no possibility that a mere ordinary individual could have an opinion of equal, let alone greater, validity than that held by the Party officials. This *cannot* happen because the Party, as the official interpreter of the Marxian gospel, has a higher wisdom. Also, because the Party is a more efficient focus for the expression of Will, and because it is the agent for furthering the accomplishment of the purposes of history according to the dialectical process.

All this smacks of a sort of modern mysticism. Indeed, it is based on an attitude towards the authority of the State—as centered in the Communist Party—that is irrational and mystic to an extreme degree. Only an examination of its philosophic roots can make such an attitude comprehensible. For, we must remember, it is not only the ordinary citizen of the Soviet Union who accepts this attitude. The Party controls not only the foreign policy and the economic life of Russia; it has absolute authority over its scientific and artistic life as well. It controls the whole "Culture" of the country, in the sense of Hegel's philosophy of the state, in the sense in which your German uses the word "Kultur."

It is hard for us to realize that to the Marxist there are no standards of right or wrong, good or evil, excellence or failure, except those which pertain to the cause of furthering his point of view. Yet we have seen repeated examples of this fact in recent years. Good music is that which increases devotion to the cause of party and state either through reference to historic events, or by stimulating the rhythm of production. Good art is that which portrays the deeds of Soviet heroes or the foibles of capitalist civilization. Correct science is that which applies the principles of the Marxian dialectic. All correspondence to any other standards is omitted, and thus all comparison with the art and science of other lands is rendered invalid and useless.

We can certainly claim far greater freedom of expression in the arts. We can also feel sure that science has with us a greater opportunity for free experiment, for developing new hypotheses, and for giving up those that no longer serve to advance our knowledge. All this is in accordance with our traditions that underwrite the greatest possible freedom for the artist and scientist without imposing on him the requirement that his achievements square with any dogmatic ideas. But in our tendency to claim moral superiority for our national policies we often appear hypocritical and indeed seem sometimes outrightly to betray the ideals we claim to champion.

We shall examine such failures to live up to our own best traditions in the closing chapter.

In the meantime we must remember that the propaganda of Marxism, despite its requirement of the acceptance of state or party authority, has great advantages in the world of today. To people whose present condition precludes freedom as we know it, the Marxist vision still has a potent lure. It puts first what such people want first—it offers economic opportunity for all men; it inveighs against colonialism under which many of them have suffered; it is unencumbered with any supernatural religion, and this appeals to peoples emerging from the mists of primitive superstition.

Of course the vision is false; the promises will not be kept. The predicted abundance will not speedily develop nor the classless society come into being. But those who have suffered an earthly hell of ignorance and exploitation will easily be misled by the offer of an earthly heaven. They will not quickly see that by accepting such an offer they will be exchanging an old subservience for a new subjection.

9

How Firm a Foundation?

THE TIME has now come to look back at the philosophic bases we have unearthed, those that support our way of life and those that support Russia's. We must ask ourselves how firm these bases are today, and to what extent they can support and direct our present policies. This inquiry, as it closes, must attempt to show again how close the relation really is between apparently abstract general principles and the most immediate and concrete questions of the day.

Remote as they may seem from the American scene of today, in spite of the fact that most of us are never brought into direct contact with them, the philosophic bases that underlie our political and social patterns are still those of Locke, of Mill, and of Hume. If we trace the origins of our attitudes, we find that they are rooted still in the concepts of man and of the state which these thinkers, Locke most of all, gave to those who founded and first shaped our nation.

We still hold it to be true that men are, or should be, free and equal "by nature." We still agree, if we think it through

together, as we have tried here to do, that man is distinguished
and characterized by his unique ability to observe and interpret his world. We can see, therefore, how necessary freedom
and equality are for the best fulfillment of this basic function
of man. We would still in theory, and so far as possible in
practice, restrict the powers of whatever government we set
up accordingly. For the purpose of such government is still
conceived as being to protect our liberties, and its scope as
being no greater than the minimum needed to accomplish
this.

This is all very fine. But, are we justified in holding fast to
these basic beliefs? After all, they were shaped in a different
age, and in a very different sort of world. To what extent are
they still sound and trustworthy? How satisfactory are the
political and social forms we have built upon the basis they
provide?

With regard to our own philosophic roots, we have already
seen that Locke's concept of the nature and function of man
was long since found wanting by later philosophers. His concepts of man as a "mental substance," of the mind as a "blank
tablet," and of mental activity as limited to receiving and
combining ideas were inadequate. Not only Kant and his followers but also most of the world's best psychologists have
found them so.

In the first place, the human mind, in the nature of which
man's real "essence" is to be found, is not a *substance;* it is a
special functioning of some elemental *energy.* Modern physics
and modern psychology would agree on that, though each
would develop many disagreements in the process of further
analysis of the mind.

In the second place, the mind, in the very process of receiving impressions, selects and orders them, and arranges
them into meaningful patterns. Just ask yourself if you really
spend much of your time merely letting impressions strike you
haphazardly. No, unless you are idly daydreaming. Otherwise

you will, even though you are not aware of it, constantly select, arrange, and interpret the impressions you receive.

One simple example will pretty well prove this. Suppose you have just got up from bed in the morning, and have gone to the window to look out. In the very act and instant of seeing how things look outside, you will single out certain impressions, combine them, interpret them in the light of what you have seen, heard, and smelled on other occasions. Even as you turn away from the window, you will already have decided what to wear to the office, or how you will spend your day of leisure, in accordance with what interpretation you have made of the impressions you have received.

The implication of this is clear, and this is the basis for most of the thinking done about the nature of the mind since the days of Hume. We need to add an active factor to our traditional concept of the nature of the human mind. This we have long since done, consciously or not. For we know, if we think about it at all, that the human mind does not merely receive and combine ideas by chance. In doing so, it is ceaselessly motivated by an urge, or instinct, to relate them to some sort of purposeful activity. The purpose of such activity is probably successful adjustment to environment. This would hold true for the simple example given above. You will probably find it holding true for any or all other examples you may think of.

But does the addition of this active, "selective" factor to our concept of man's mind, of his essential nature, destroy our traditional basis for believing in the freedom and equality of men? There is no reason why it should do so. Whether they are made by instinct or by conscious choice, the decisions of living organisms are usually directed toward coping successfully with their environment. The bird "decides" to fly south—in order that its food supply may not fail. You decide to become a doctor or a carpenter—in order that you may best adjust yourself to your environment, and, it is true, also that your food supply may not fail.

But, in the case of the *conscious* decision, your personal freedom of choice is, or seems at the moment, completely real. Mark that it is most important that this be the case, and that you may feel "free" at the moment of choice. For you may turn out to be the best doctor or the best carpenter the world has ever known. Thus, to increase the possibilities for unprecedented excellence in all fields, men should have freedom of choice and equality of opportunity to develop their talents, so as to make the best and most useful adjustment to the environment in which they live.

In other words, the addition of a new "active" factor to our old concept of man's nature implies no limitation on the freedom and equality of all men. In fact, it even gives strong additional reason for the development of political and social patterns that will protect these "rights" and will underwrite their "unalienable" character. Progress in all forms of life depends upon the possibility of new patterns of adjustment; such patterns can develop in human society only if the way is kept open, by safeguarding man's freedom, for constant individual variation.

This truth of itself refutes any theory of the "absolute state," any authority which can order not only men's lives, but also compel conformity to an official point of view.

So far our philosophic premises may be sound enough. But do we have to recognize the fact that, in our present world, a measure of restraint upon the freedom of men may be necessary in terms of actual social practice? Indeed we do.

At this point, we may well recall that Locke himself foresaw that such social restraints might become necessary. To him it seemed clear that there was "land enough in the world to suffice double the number of inhabitants." But this is no longer true. Double—and quadruple—the number of inhabitants we now have. For Locke, there was enough space so that each industrious individual could separate from "the common wild" what land and resources he could make his own through his labor. But Locke added that he could do this "at least where there is enough, and as good, left in common for others." Today, there isn't. Even in our own continent, which looked to Locke so inexhaustible, we are appalled at the impoverishment of our land, and the despoliation of our resources. As we note this shameful waste of our natural wealth, we may well remember that Locke said, of those very resources of nature, "Nothing was made by God for man to spoil and destroy."

It is important for us to realize that we can find, within our own philosophic heritage, a perfectly sound basis for placing restrictions upon the unbridled functioning of "rugged individualism" and "free enterprise." Locke himself supplies this. The means must be consent of the majority; the goal must be the maintenance of the greatest possible freedom and equality for all under current conditions.

Under such limitations, the taking of steps needed to restrain individual freedom is merely a reapplication of our traditional principles. There is certainly nothing "Un-American" in placing restraints upon the individual, by consent of the majority, so that all may more securely enjoy, under existing circumstances, the greatest possible measure of "life, liberty, and the pursuit of happiness." Our philosophic bases can adjust themselves to the needs of the moment without violation of the principles of government we have derived from them.

It is only when we, who are steeped in our own philosophic heritage of freedom, come to believe that state controls are desirable *as an end in themselves* that we deny our birthright. For then we are in danger of succumbing to the paralyzing doctrine that "the state knows best," which leads so easily to the concept of the state as endowed with "higher wisdom." That concept is indeed "Un-American." For it remains the task of the United States to explore and explain the reasons why the individual should have all possible freedom, and to champion those forms of government which will best protect that freedom.

We should note here that the need to add an active, purposeful factor to our concept of man's mind does have an important effect on our heritage from Hume. For we can no longer accept his view of the mind as a mere sensitive plate upon which sense impressions and their associated feelings write their record. This removes the philosophic ground for the economic theories based on Hume's view of the mind. Here Marx was right. The first factor to be considered, in forming a theory of economics, is not the hypothetical "sum total of happiness" which expanding production may bring. It is the actual conditions under which the labor is performed which make such production possible.

Thus we can clear the way for an economic doctrine which accepts many limitations on the old "laissez-faire" theory which was based on Hume. Such limitations will be designed to protect proper labor conditions, and equal rights for labor and management alike. But, in forming such a theory, the rights of *all* must be considered, not merely those of one "class," too sharply, and quite falsely, set off from all others.

We can see that our philosophic bases for true *freedom of the individual* remain sound and trustworthy, even though those on which complete *freedom of enterprise* rested may have to be somewhat shifted in the interests of a satisfactory economic life. In fact, this must be done if we are to meet the challenge of the alleged "people's democracy" supposedly offered by the Soviet Union. Already we have made long strides toward doing so, for we have achieved a democracy in which the interests of all groups can be expressed and made influential.

Now we must turn to those philosophic premises which underlie the political and social regime of the Soviet Union. How well have they fared in the light of later thought? How trustworthy are they as support for future political and social forms?

We had better begin by repeating that the most fundamental of these premises, Kant's "answer to Hume," his concept of the mind of man as active, is correct. It is necessary for any true understanding of the mind. The trouble began, the ground for dangerous doctrine was laid, when one type of its activity, that of *willing,* was singled out as that which was basically characteristic of man, and its other activities, thinking and feeling, were lost sight of. With Fichte, this activity of *will* became the one, all-inclusive characteristic of human nature. Thus a function, a type of activity, which man shares with all animal life was taken to be his distinguishing characteristic. This at once can be seen to be a misleading concept. Man is a willful being, true. But that is not what is unique about him. His unique nature, his "essence," can much better be taken to be either, as in the medieval picture, his quality of being the focus of God's purpose here on earth, or, in the picture from the Age of Enlightenment, as given by Locke, his quality of being the observer and interpreter of the natural world.

Thus we find an immediate flaw in the premises which have given rise to totalitarian views.

Moreover, Fichte held that man, being Will Incarnate, must find that the expression of will is his natural function. Such expression, said Fichte, must take the form of struggle to overcome opposition. The *Self* must always be struggling against the *Not-Self,* that is, everything outside itself. But why? Man's will can equally well be directed toward harmonizing his interests with those of his fellows. There *is* a strongly aggressive streak in human nature. But there is an equally natural tendency toward co-operation. If Fichte had recognized this, if, to the struggle of the self with the not-self, he had added the adjustment of the self to other selves, he would have provided a far safer, as well as a far sounder, basis for political theories.

Unfortunately, he did not do so. What "adjustment" there had to be was left to the state, which, as you will remember, was thought of as superior to the individual because it was a more efficient focus for the working of the will. Again here, if Fichte had only added the tendency to co-operate to the tendency to overcome, his philosophy of the state would have been far less dangerous. Especially so, since he held that the rights of individuals were theirs merely so that they could the better do their duty by the state! Fichte's theory thus has led to the belief that the citizen's duty to the state has much more to do with helping that state to overcome others than it does with helping it to co-operate with others. Thus it is hard for any nation that has much of Fichte in its philosophic heritage to co-operate in an international system such as the United Nations.

We should mark well here that the basic fallacy to be found in the philosophic bases of the Soviet Union is that man is a being primarily characterized by an aggressive will which he can best exercise by giving absolute power to a state—or a Party.

When we come to examine the elements which Hegel added to the foundations of totalitarianism, we find other and even more alarming fallacies. The first one is that which we discussed at some length before, the concept of the state as the revelation of the "Divine Idea" on earth. We must point again to the grave danger of this particularly repugnant theory. Not only did it underlie the ominous growth of Imperial Germany, and the mounting frenzy of Nazism; it is today one of the chief philosophic supports of the policies of the Soviet Union. Yet there is certainly nothing in the record of history which, to an unbiased intelligence, indicates that the state, as such, has ever acted in this capacity—most surely never a state founded on the idea of men as vehicles of an aggressive will. Indeed, it has been this very idea, translated into terms of armed power, which has been the motivating force behind the ruin and tragedy of two World Wars.

We must mention one more basic fallacy in the philosophic background of the totalitarian state. That is the "Dialectic," which, in its "materialistic" form, is the backbone of Marxist theory. Marx, you will recall, though an atheist, and an avowed foe of all that was mystic and occult, completely accepted this theory of progress only through violent clash and relentless struggle. There is little if any evidence, on the basis of objective, unbiased observation, that the dialectic pattern prevails in any field of scientific inquiry. You can say, of course, that an excess of one sort sometimes brings an excess of its opposite. But that is about all you can claim for this method of the dialectic in actual history. Moreover, in science, one idea does not often give way to its opposite through one clear-cut clash. The idea that the sun, not the earth, is the center of the universe existed for centuries before it was accepted. It overcame the other view slowly and gradually, not by a sudden shock of violent opposition. The theory of organic evolution, introduced by Darwin, has never been violently overthrown, but it has been modified and greatly changed. This is the sort of process by which ideas, theories, and systems *really* develop: but a course of gradual growth and adaptation, not by "revolutionary" overturn.

The basic trouble with the premises of Marxism is that the German philosophers, in whose thinking it is rooted, brought in the idea that progress comes only through *struggle, opposition, overcoming,* not, as our mentors had held, through gradual and orderly *growth.*

There are other things we can say about the "Dialectic." We might dare to remark that it is just about as "scientifically" based as is the theory of "astral influence" on our characters and lives. Or, we may note, with interest, that, to whatever extent change does come about through opposition, there is no reason to believe that any thesis has only *one* antithesis, indeed, there may be any number. The land owners of the medieval period *could* have been succeeded by the peasants, or by the clergy, as the ruling class; it didn't *have* to be the bourgeoisie. The bourgeois state, if it falls, can be succeeded by various kinds of other states; it does not *have* to be by "proletarian democracy." There is no reason, apart from blind dogmatism, to hold that the present Soviet state is the perfect and final form of society, or that Marx, Engels, Lenin, Stalin, and Khrushchev have given all the answers.

We should note here, too, that even if the dialectic process were fundamental in all things, as the Marxist is taught to believe, Marx would still have been wrong in teaching that once the proletarian revolution had occurred the process would cease. We have already seen that such a revolution, like any other, is almost certain to substitute one ruling class for another. You cannot, as Lenin taught, cure the class struggle by intensifying it. You can do so only by gradual easing of its tensions. Any supposedly temporary "dictatorship of the proletariat" is almost certain to petrify into the hard core of an enduring bureaucracy. Therefore, the same elements of social conflict will continue to operate. In terms of his own beloved Dialectic, were Marx living, he would have to admit that the Soviet state, which, as we saw, has developed a new ruling class, has become a new "thesis" for which the proper "antithesis" must be found.

We are justified in dwelling a little bit on the Marxist's insistence that his approach to social problems is the only "scientific" one. Vishinsky repeats this over and over again. He bases his claim on the "fact" that his approach is the only one that avoids "abstractions." That is, Vishinsky holds, all "bourgeois" ideas of the state, of law, etc., are based on general bourgeois concepts of "the will of the people," truth, justice, human rights, etc. The Marxist says these are unreal abstractions which do not really exist. There exists only the class struggle; that alone is real. For example, Vishinsky says of law that it exists merely to express "the social relationship between classes on the basis of the domination, repression, and subjection, by the dominant classes, of the other classes which are subordinated to this dominance."

This is said to be the only scientific approach to an understanding of how law operates in the state. Yet anyone not muddled by Marxism may well fail to understand why such extreme and unnatural separation of society into classes is not just as much and just as vicious a case of abstraction as the formulation of general concepts of truth, and of justice.

Throughout his history man has dreamed and wrought in terms of the very concepts which Vishinsky is deriding. They are surely as real in the story of humanity as the later concepts of class and struggle and hatred. The "abstractions" of truth, honor, and justice have bound men together in many a brave attempt to build a better world. Whether they exist in the very stars, as Plato thought, or only in the minds of men, such concepts have always been the leaven of all human endeavor.

The later "abstractions" of class struggle are today setting men against each other, and thus preventing progress towards a better life.

This brings us to the gravest defect in the premises of Karl Marx himself. Marx never gave us a concept of the nature of man as *man*. To him, men were so sharply differentiated into classes that they were primarily characterized as members of this or that *class*. They were lacking in a common human nature. Each man is supposed to be characterized by one sort of class consciousness. But there is no inclusive concept of all men as *man,* a being distinguished by *human* consciousness. One is to think of himself as a member of the proletariat, or of the bourgeoisie, not as a member of the human race. Marx supplied, that is, no unifying concept to take the place of that which had marked men as members of one great Christian community. Unlike Christ, Marx did not preach the brotherhood of all men, only of the members of the "working class." His attitude may remind us of that of the Nazi propagandist who besought his countrymen to think of themselves "first as Germans, second only as human beings."

This same background, which is so closely related to Fichte, and to his doctrine of the ceaseless struggle of the will, underlay the thinking of Marx. Obsessed as he understandably was with the cruel suffering of the workers of his time, he left us no legacy of a concept of man in which all of the alleged classes can discover a common humanity.

Christianity was founded on the love of man for man; Marxism on the hatred of class for class.

Right here we should again face the fact that it has been these very philosophic premises which we have been unearthing in this study which have supported the political forms, the attitudes and prejudices, of the two nations which have, in recent times, offered the greatest threat to the free society of the western world—Germany and Russia. Different as each is from the other, both, in their forms and patterns of life, were impregnated by the ideas of Fichte and Hegel, which extolled the superiority of the state to the individual, which counselled the citizen to merge his will with that of the state, and which absolved the state from the common canons of morality.

Only an understanding of the philosophic premises of Germany and Soviet Russia makes the fearful history of the last half-century at all intelligible. From those premises have been derived the theories of total war, of state espionage, new "elite" classes, the concentration camps, and slave labor. Indirectly from these same sources, as a perhaps necessary counterpart, has come, in large measure, the breakdown in national morality of those lands which have opposed the totalitarian states. The result of this has been, for example, our own acceptance of merciless warfare, "area bombing," the use of the atom bomb on civilian centers, and other practices of which we of the West may well be ashamed.

The free society of the West will never be secure so long as any great and heavily armed state exists which draws its motivations from the philosophic foundations of Fichte and Hegel. Although most of us were not aware of it, that was the deepest and most basic danger in Germany's two attempts at European, and perhaps world, domination. Today, we sense the same threat in the aggressiveness of the Soviet Union. But let us not make the mistake of thinking that Russia, not Germany, has always been our real danger. Today, for example, many blame Franklin Roosevelt for not seeing this. But his mistake was not in opposing Germany under Hitler to the bitter end. It was in believing that Stalin would play fair if he were well treated. Roosevelt made the same mistake about Stalin that Chamberlain made about Hitler. Each failed to realize that the man he was up against could not be treated as though his thought and action were drawn from the same philosophic sources as his own.

In one way the Soviet Union today seems to threaten far less than did Germany under Hitler, or, in a less virulent form, under Wilhelm II. Marxism does not extoll and glorify war. Marxism does not preach the superiority of any one race, or its right to trample on the rights of others. The Soviet Union wishes to avoid war, and will do so if possible. But she is preparing the way, if war becomes necessary for her, by trying to make men believe that, if war occurs, it will be the fault of the "capitalist imperialists."

Even though she may try to avoid the use of outright, armed force in attaining her ends, the Soviet Union is driven by a compulsion no less dynamic than was Germany's to spread her power, influence, and control. In doing so, she offers a different, but no less alarming, threat to the world. Its danger lies in the fact that wherever men are in misery, and oppression, and ignorance, they may turn to Russia's dream of a classless society with abundance for all the workers. If their need is enough, they may do so without counting the cost in human dignity or in freedom, without realizing the new form of slavery to the state which the Soviet Union today demands. For no pressure group in a "bourgeois" society, no "special interests," can so enslave and degrade men today as can the power of the total state in the service of the all-powerful Communist Party.

We need not doubt that Marx sincerely wanted to improve the conditions of life for the exploited and oppressed. We can understand that Lenin sincerely hoped to create in the Soviet Union a state where a better life could be found. But our examination of the philosophic foundations of their theories should show us that these can never provide that better life.

To set one class of men against all others can never bring happiness to them. To attempt to set up a classless society by force and violence will always fail. To deprive men of their human birthright to think for themselves will always leave them dissatisfied. To determine what each man must do will not result either in satisfaction or a high level of production. All this we have known for some time.

Now, however, we can see that the deepest reasons for such failures lie in the fact that they are the result of the application of theories based on a wrong concept of the nature of man. Man is a creature of will, yes. But he is also endowed with reason, and he may well also feel himself to be the focus of some cosmic purpose. Any way of life that denies him the right to use the one for himself, and to speculate as to the other, will not bring him dignity, self-respect, or satisfaction with his way of life.

10

Freedom, Peace, and Power

OUR INQUIRY has shown us the persistent strength of our own philosophic foundations and the reasons for believing that—with certain additions and adaptations—they can still support a successful society in the contemporary world. It has shown also the dangerous misconceptions on which rest the philosophic foundations of the Soviet Union, as well as its political, economic, and social organization. Can the inquiry also help us to determine the policies proper for us in the present period of tension and recurrent crisis? If it can, its method must be to uphold those policies that square with our traditions and philosophic heritage, and to decry those that betray that heritage. For only thus can we feel certain that we are proving to the world that our concepts of man and of the state have more to offer to mankind than do those of the systems that oppose us.

We stand in need of such certainty today in the struggle for world leadership between the United States and the Soviet Union. That struggle, all too familiar to us as the cold war, is being waged the world over in economic and local military conflict. Tomorrow or the day after it may erupt at any number of focal points into outright battle, which all too easily could "escalate" overnight into general war. The current "balance of terror," the knowledge that no nation could possibly win such a war, will not save us forever. It is indeed a matter of life or death for millions of us to examine all means of maintaining peace. What light can our philosophic heritage throw upon this essential endeavor?

The United States was born out of the interaction of a certain concept of man—one that held him to be the independent, rational observer, and interpreter of his world—and of the marvelous opportunity of settling and developing a whole new continent. From that interaction of philosophic and natural factors was engendered the form of our government and the pattern of our way of life. Out of it too has grown the complex of our typical attitudes, prejudices, and practices.

Freedom of the individual remains the touchstone of our instinctive concern and its protection the goal of government. We talk in terms of maintaining a "free society" at home and of sustaining the "Free World" elsewhere. It is natural and indeed inevitable for us to do so because of our philosophic heritage. But to what extent do our present policies really sustain our own best traditions? To what extent are we really underwriting the essentials of freedom at home and abroad?

We had best first consider the degree to which we are maintaining, or failing to maintain, the traditions of our heritage here at home. We have built the world's most affluent society; more of us live in a greater measure of comfort than men have at any time or in any region. But is our society today really the embodiment of the principles, dreams, and hopes of those who founded it? And is it still worthy to serve as a magnet for mankind's aspirations for a better future?

In assaying our assets and liabilities as the champions of freedom, we must first face that worst blight on our body politic—our continuing reluctance to grant our Negro citizens their full measure of real equality. Nothing so damages our image abroad, nothing so sickens our own conscience, as this failure to live up the promises of the past. Despite the recent decisions of the Supreme Court and the Civil Rights Act, the dead weight of prejudice still stultifies progress toward eradicating this stain upon our national honor.

Jefferson foresaw that slavery was wrong and that all our citizens must be free. For a century all have been free in name. But after one hundred years of "freedom" more than one tenth of our fellow Americans are treated as second-class citizens if, indeed, they are allowed the prerogatives of citizenship at all. In many states there is only token integration in the schools, in some hardly any. In many states only a fraction of Negroes are registered voters. Nor is the South by any means wholly to blame. Social segregation prevails in all parts of our "free" nation.

Segregation wounds those who are segregated. But it also causes a psychological malaise among those who impose it in a nation whose philosophic traditions require equality. For they know—even though they will not admit it—that true equality is not to be found so long as segregation persists. Wherever such a discrepancy between philosophic heritage and actual practice exists, a sick conscience is the result.

Moreover the practice of segregation, for which all Americans are to blame, makes a mockery of our claim to champion freedom in the eyes of the awakening African nations. It is no wonder that thousands of young Africans who would otherwise prefer to study here are turning to Russia and other Communist countries for their education. We could have found no surer way to lose the leadership of the future than by this

maintenance of racial prejudice at home. Herein lies our greatest failure to realize the true implications of our philosophic
heritage.

But there are other if less spectacular ways in which we are
failing to live up to our historic promise to champion freedom.
We tend, for instance, to confuse resistance to "socialistic
ideas" with the protection of the real freedom of the individual.
If this seems inevitable it is nevertheless unfortunate. Franklin
Roosevelt was cursed for introducing "socialism" when he
established a measure of governmental control of business. But
it may well be true that only by such steps was an eventual
violent revolution prevented and all that could be maintained
of capitalist society preserved. Social Security was bitterly resisted at first; now we would not dispense with it if we could.
At present medical care for the aged is being resisted; within
a decade we may wonder how we got along without it. Such
steps that the complexity and changing nature of our society
make necessary do not always make a man less free. Certainly
helplessness and dependence on others do more to crush the
spirit of freedom. Surely too, any tendency to stifle originality,
to compel conformity, and to punish non-conformance do so.
The Scandinavian countries are highly "socialized" but the
measure in which the individual is free to think and indeed to
behave as he chooses is often higher than it is with us. All the
resurgent countries of western Europe have long had a mixed
economy, part free, part controlled, and yet in most of them
the air of freedom prevails as much or often far more than
here. It is a hard lesson but one that must be learned—that
some yielding to a measure of socialism is the only way a free
society can successfully resist the pressures that otherwise may
well insure the spread of communism.

Again, the pressure to conform does not come from our
true philosophic heritage. It is far more closely related to the
lingering vestiges of Puritanism that, whatever its virtues may
have been, left a legacy of suspicion of the "different" indi-

vidual that was wholly alien to the traditions of the Age of Enlightenment. Indeed such a tendency has far more in common with the traditions of a totalitarian social order. This pressure to conform, this resentment against those who deviate from "normal" patterns of thought, has done and is doing far more to limit individual freedom than any amount of "socialistic" legislation that could conceivably come into being in our nation today. But in all fairness it should be pointed out that this tendency is shared with that other world whose traditions are the opposite of ours and whose methods of enforcing conformity are far more effective. Perhaps that is why the phenomena of revolt among the young are so frequent in both the "free" and the Communist worlds.

But even if we in these ways fail to maintain our traditions of freedom do we not at least steadfastly support "freedom of enterprise"? We have already pointed out that in the industrial field the development of a complex and crowded society has made some governmental controls necessary and will undoubtedly necessitate more. But here too there are other than governmental pressures at work to weaken our old tradition. There are few among us today who do not realize that real freedom of enterprise as our forefathers conceived it, the ability of the small operator to engage in competitive business, has been ebbing rapidly and at an ever increasing pace. The reason for this is all too obvious and it is not interference by government; it is the smothering effect of the machinations of "big business." Combinations, mergers, monopolies, are far more effective in terms of efficiency of operation and of profits. In all fields, from that of mass media to that of dairy farming, it is the same story—the trend is toward the pooling of money and power. All too often those who talk loudest about the sanctity of freedom of enterprise are the very ones who are doing their best to stifle it by making enterprise impossible for the small operator. It may be that these tendencies are inevitable and irreversible, but, if so, it is a misuse of terms to label them the continuance of the tradition of freedom of enterprise. They represent a departure from that tradition far more threatening to the health of a free society than any regulation by government of business practices. Or, as we said earlier, by any threat from the Communist world.

We have now listed and criticized several of the ways in which we fail to maintain the heritage of freedom that we derive from our philosophic foundations and by which we endanger here at home our chances of being accepted by the world as champions of freedom. Now what about the ways in which we endanger—or inhibit—that reputation by our practices abroad? How do we look to others when we pose as the chief supporter of what we like to think of as the Free World? Here is to be found the focal point of the dislike and suspicion with which we are so often regarded and that we resent and find hard to understand.

The United States has given away more of its resources than any nation in all history. Its people have sincerely wanted to aid others, to alleviate their suffering, to rehabilitate them after war and disaster, to establish the economic viability of new nations whose independence could not possibly be maintained without our assistance. In doing all this we have been prompted by our real and ready sympathy and by our sincere desire to help others toward freedom. In this we are sustained by the best traditions of our philosophic heritage that instill into us a seemingly innate desire to assist others toward the sort of life we prize and preach. Why then are we regarded with reactions that vary from indifference to hostility, instead of with appreciation and friendship?

Of course it is clear that in part the hostile reactions of many parts of the world toward us are due to Communist propaganda that represents us always as rapacious, hypocritical "imperialists." But this is not all there is to the story of our failure to win friends around the world by our generosity and offers of protection and assistance. In the first place, the Free-

World mystique we have tried to create and sustain just does not sell very well in many parts of the earth. Too often it seems that in the name of freedom we are either protecting our own strategic position or maintaining in power regimes that willingly cooperate with either our military or economic interests. Take Taiwan (Formosa) as an example. It is true that the presence of our military might protects—and must protect—it from absorption by China. That fact is widely understood and widely accepted in much of the Far East. But why must we complicate the matter and alienate many who would like to be our friends by claiming that Taiwan is a bastion of the Free World. It is in reality a police state ruled by a ruthless dictator who is kept in control merely because of our support. In Vietnam we are trying to overcome the activities of the Communist Vietcong by supporting regimes that are distinctly unpopular with the masses of its long suffering inhabitants. In much of Latin America, in Spain, in Portugal, we are all too ready to give aid and support to governments that cannot even by the wildest stretch of imagination be classed as free.

If the United States would talk in terms of its own military and political necessities, its own security, we would be listened to with respect if not with affection. But to state our policies in terms of protecting freedom makes us appear as hypocrites and undermines the confidence of many peoples in our fitness for world leadership. It does little good for us to add that we are protecting them against communism when they see that our protection means the maintenance in power of a ruling clique, as well as the entrenched prerogatives of a few wealthy families underwritten by church and state. They know all too well the hardships of their present situation; they cannot foresee those that communism would undoubtedly force upon them. In the meantime we appear as their enemies rather than as their friends.

In addition to the resentment engendered by this "enforced" military assistance, there is also the widespread feeling that we have too often encouraged American big business to make profits in undeveloped lands without regard for their inhabitants. While we have not been colonialists in the technical sense, we have enjoyed the same advantages through the ruthless exploitation of resources that should have to some degree benefited the peoples of the lands in which they were found. Nor has it seemed very often to matter to us with what sort of regime we have dealt so long as no obstacles were put in the path of our profits. Perhaps the prime example of this today is the way in which American business is involved in the exploitation of the mineral wealth of the Union of South Africa. The benefits incurred are certainly not shared by those segregated under the system of *apartheid* nor by the detachments of forced labor recruited from Portugal's anachronistic neighboring colonies.

All this would not matter so much if we did not constantly profess ideals that we so often fail to practice. But for almost two centuries the peoples of this earth, as they have become aware of our existence, have been drawn toward us and have put their trust in us because of the shining dream of liberty and equality that we have seemed to embody. Now, just as the media of instant communication and overnight travel bring all the world together, we seem to many not to be living up to that dream nor to the hopes that it has for so long engendered in the hungry heart of mankind.

It makes our tragedy even more unfortunate to realize that we do not need to look elsewhere than to our own best traditions to remedy this. As we have seen, and as we shall further review, our own deepest foundations, our philosophic wellsprings, still have more to offer to men than have those of our adversaries.

But it is time now to turn our attention to the record of those who oppose us, who compete for the role of standard bearers for the hopes of man. How have their patterns of behavior accorded with the promises they have made of a better future for those who follow their lead? With what degree of success have they created a better environment for men in their own land and in the countries they control?

To the workers of the world Karl Marx promised that their seizure of power would bring into being a new internationalized society free of all class distinction and the curse of war, which was always the fault of capitalism. After him, Lenin insisted that such a society could be established in Russia even if, because of the dying struggles of the capitalist world and its implacable enmity, the vision of a peaceful world engaged in the creation of communism could not at once be realized. It fell to Joseph Stalin, as Lenin's chosen heir, to supervise the organization of a socialist society in Russia that would progress as rapidly as possible to the establishment of communism. In the process, a classless society would come into being, all the oppressions and injustices of capitalism would be eliminated, and gradually the state as organized power would, in the words of Engels, "wither away."

We know, and the whole world knows, that this has not happened. Oppression and injustice most certainly were not eliminated by Stalin and while amelioration has developed under Khrushchev, the citizens of the Soviet Union are far less free than are those of many capitalist lands. Moreover, no classless society has come into being. On the contrary a new ruling class, a bureaucratic *élite,* is in power and shows not the slightest tendency to relinquish its control. The nature and practices of this new class were well described by Milovan Djilas, and no evidence of its disappearance is to be found in any other report on conditions in Russia. This could, and should, have been foreseen. Those who hold power are always reluctant to relinquish it. Where power has been won by force, as it was in Russia in 1917, it is force alone that can overthrow it so long as the means of peaceful change, free elections and a truly representative legislative authority, are forbidden to a people. Djilas, in speaking of the three stages of the building of a Com-

munist state says, "In the revolution it was necessary to seize
power; in the building of socialism it was necessary to create
a new system by means of that power; today power must preserve the system."

The state has not withered away; the Party has *become* the
State and its leaders have no intention of stepping down from
their privileged positions. The "vanguard of the proletariat"
intends to keep the people under its firm control. It may now
permit them a greater or smaller measure of freedom as conditions change within and outside their nation, but it is the Party
and not the people who will decide what is best.

Nor do we need to confine our criticism of Russia's failure
to achieve a classless society to such generalities. There are
too many reports, official and otherwise, of the inequalities
prevalent in the Soviet Union for us to be in any doubt. Klaus
Mehnert in his *Soviet Man* gives many good and often amus-
ing examples. In one he records the reactions and remarks of
women shoppers at the great G.U.M. store in Moscow on seeing the wives of party officials leaving their limousines to enter
the boutique of an expensive Paris couturier across the street.
Mehnert speaks also of the frequency with which the regime
is referred to as "They" by the ordinary citizen—always a
sign of a sense of impotence in the face of authority.

There are also countless reports of the dissatisfaction of the
young people of Russia and of the disillusionment of many of
the intellectuals of the country. Their initial revolutionary enthusiasm has evaporated not only because the application of
Marxian theories has failed to produce the promised society
but because they now doubt its very dogmas. Indifference or
hostility mark the reactions of many to official propaganda.
The cause is, however, more to be found in the failure of the
system to produce a society of abundance than in any wish to
overturn the regime. Mehnert reports that he once asked a
local official, who was complaining about the central government, if he did not wish for more freedom. The man replied:

"Anything but that!" The philosophic foundations of Marxism still make men fearful of individual freedom that, they fear, will lead directly to political anarchy.

Even so, there is no doubt that there is great concern among the Russian "ruling circles" over the falling away of faith that marks contemporary youth in their country. In *A New Russia?* Harrison Salisbury quotes a middle-aged party official as saying: "This is our greatest defeat—the young people have deserted the cause. I do not know how we are going to get them back." It is probable that this increasing skepticism is one of the main reasons why the Soviet Union exaggerates out of all proportion the danger of encirclement and attack by the "aggressors of the West." The specter of a threat from outside a nation is so often raised to induce loyalty within it. But it is doubtful that the young people of Russia who have deserted the cause will be won back by this technique. The fact that their faith has wavered would indicate that they no longer are impressed by the Marxian axiom of the inevitability of capitalist attack.

There can be no doubt, moreover, that economically the system of the Soviet Union is just not working very well. Standards of living have improved a great deal. But despite Khrushchev's glowing promises they have by no means approached those of the United States, and they are falling further and further behind those of the Common Market countries of western Europe. In particular the agricultural economy of Russia has failed lamentably to meet requirements, and its failure has been bitterly and repeatedly criticized by Khrushchev himself.

It cannot be hidden from the people of Russia that capitalism is by no means on its last legs. Its refusal to behave according to Marx's predictions has, of course, many causes. It can be justly claimed that it still draws strength from the vestiges of colonialism, the exploitation of the underdeveloped lands. This continues even though political control has ostensibly been withdrawn, as in Katanga where the Union Minière still dominates the local scene or in the "banana republics" of Central America where the United Fruit Company has long wielded undue influence. But, although vested interests are still strong, there is within the capitalist countries themselves a growing resentment against these practices. And within those countries the predictions of Marx about capitalism have simply not worked out. The "ruling circles," while still powerful, now have to match their might with that of organized labor and do not always prevail. In the United States and in western Europe, it has not been true that a few would grow richer while the misery of the masses increased. On the contrary, wealth is being gradually distributed more and more widely, and the interest of more and more people is centered in the preservation and improvement of the sort of mixed private and public economy that the West finds best suited for the world of today. There is very little chance of a revolution of the proletariat in the Western world. Unfortunately, change by any other means still seems almost impossible in many other regions, and where improvement of social conditions is resisted, communism is all too apt to prevail. It is true today that the rich nations get richer and the poor underdeveloped and overpopulated nations poorer. It would be ironic indeed if the Marxian prophecy of increasing disproportion of wealth, though not fulfilled within the western nations, were to work out all too fully in the world as a whole!

We should note that the expected unity of the Communist world has not continued. Marx thought that the proletariat of all lands would unite in "throwing off their chains." Later, when Stalin held that there could be a development of socialism in one country, he still insisted that there be one center for its leadership and for its continuance into true communism. But since his time, discord has disrupted the unity of thought and practice for which Moscow was supposed to remain the center. Yugoslavia has gone its own way; Albania has rebelled; China is far from obedient; and outbreaks of dissatisfaction have troubled the nations of eastern Europe. Nor is the capitalist world drawing closer to unity while the world of communism is threatening to come apart. France has disrupted the western alliance, the necessity of recognizing China splits our allegiances, the world becomes more a kaleidoscope of shifting policies than a clear opposition of two blocs of power.

The faults and failures of communism can be hidden from the ignorant and uneducated masses of many lands for whom its appeal is strong. But they cannot long remain unknown by the leaders of those lands. We have already seen evidence of this in the Near East, and we are beginning to see it in Africa. In Egypt, Nasser has proclaimed socialism but on his own terms, terms designed for the particular needs of his long suffering nation. Leaders of some of the new West African countries while opposing our often stupid insistence on adopting the forms of "democratic capitalism," want no dictation of the forms of their socialist economies from Moscow either.

Overseas the image of Russia has thus been tarnished as has our own. To picture her as the champion of a new and classless society is becoming unconvincing. She still does have a great advantage over us in that we are inextricably associated with the machinations of the colonial powers while she is not. Furthermore, what she seems to offer is "newer" than the patterns of social organization we recommend and try to institute. Our patterns are associated, however wrongly, with past oppressions and exploitations. Those of communism will undoubtedly bring new difficulties and unknown burdens. But men always recoil more readily from risking the continuance of past troubles than from those that may lie ahead of them.

The wave of independence that now washes around the world cannot be dammed by the dikes of the past. It was not communism that originated that wave. Its chief source was Woodrow Wilson's restatement of an old principle—the self determination of peoples. That principle swept Europe after the first World War; after the second it engulfed the earth. Independence—"Uhuru"—has become the focus of faith for the peoples of Africa; it has acquired a mystical significance and appears as a panacea for their past sufferings. The leaders of the new nations there and elsewhere know that massive economic aid will be necessary to establish the basis for real freedom. But they want to make their independence real, not a new form of subservience under which economic tutelage is substituted for outright political control. They will often accept any assistance they can get, but they are unwilling to permit such acceptance to carry with it the right to dictate forms of economic—or indeed of social—development. The lessons of the loss of true independence by those nations "protected against capitalist reactionaries" by Russia is not lost upon them. Nor do they fail to see how often we protect fascist regimes in the name of "preserving democracy." If we appear more hypocritical than they, it is because our traditions should bind us to tell the truth whereas for the Communist anything that furthers his cause is "true."

Two main points remain still to be discussed. Does the nature of their philosophic foundations indicate that war between the Western and Communist worlds is sooner or later inevitable? And which of those two foundations will best support not only the hope of avoiding such a war—if it is not inevitable —and best serve the aspiration of mankind for a better future? To those questions the conclusion of our inquiry must now be addressed.

First then, what light does our examination of the philosophic bases of communism throw on the haunting question of the inevitability of war? We know that Lenin held that war with the capitalist world would sooner or later occur. His belief in this was founded partly on the unfortunate and abortive military intervention by the Western Powers in an attempt to overthrow the government he had established. But it was founded in part also on the doctrinal conviction that the capitalist world would be driven by the irresistible logic of history to gather its waning forces for the destruction of the new order of society. Later, as we know, the doctrine of "coexistence" was officially substituted and is the professed basis of Russia's policies today. Its acceptance or rejection is the chief point at issue in the current tension between Moscow and Peiping.

But has coexistence really been accepted as a doctrine, or is it merely a technique that seems useful for the present period but that would be discarded overnight if and when the Communist world is certain that its strength is far greater than that of any combination of powers opposing it? That is a question to which it is impossible to get an honest answer, impossible because only an indoctrinated Marxist privy to the projects of the Kremlin could give it. And such a man would assure us that the intent behind the idea of coexistence is sincere, even if he knew it were not, because to him, of course, what is true is what best serves the interests of the cause.

Nevertheless all the evidence we can gather indicates that whether or not there has been any real amending of dogma, the Soviet Union will not at present press the cold war into outright worldwide conflict by deliberate intent. Apparently a dichotomy has developed between what are practical courses of action and what remain axiomatic principles. The magazine *Kommunist* said in June, 1962: "Reasonable mutual concessions in the interests of peace are natural in relations among states but it is *unnatural* to try to apply that principle to the ideological struggle." And the same article added, "Peaceful coexistence does not mean the relaxation of the ideological struggle."

Now it is exactly at this point that our examination of the philosophical roots of Marxism can help us most. For it explains the readiness of the representatives of Russia to meet in any number of conferences, to spin out endlessly the process of debate and then to arrive at no acceptable formula for settlement.

It thus becomes clearer than ever that further attempts at

honest negotiations with the Soviet Union will almost certainly prove fruitless. No arguments, however fair, no compromises however reasonable, will be of any permanent avail. The true Marxist believes in the "historic" rightness of his cause and therefore cannot really accept the principles of "conference procedure," which are second nature to the peoples of the West. We should make the basic realization that your devout Marxist is just as convinced of the rightness of his "faith" as were the priests who accompanied Cortez to Mexico. To expect him to compromise his point of view with ours is to be as unrealistic as it would have been to look for a compromise between the Jesuits and the Aztec priests. This may seem like an absurdly extreme statement. But, the more one seeks to understand the attitude of the devoted Marxist, the more he sees it as the secular projection of suppressed religious conviction. No wonder that the Catholic Church calls Marxism the greatest secular heresy in history. Both are "absolutisms"; but the Church claims to restrict its authority to one field of man's interests even though it does not always do so. Both fear rebellious opinion, which one calls heresy, the other deviationism.

Our inquiry shows us the deepest reasons for the unyielding character of the Marxist approach. That approach derives from the belief that man's true function as a creature of will is to *overcome opposition*. Distant as its origins are, manifold as are the connecting links in the history of thought, the Communist thinks of his world as a "Self" in the Fichtean sense and of our world as that "Not-self," which must be overwhelmed.

If all this is true, if we now have exposed the deepest reason why negotiations will not succeed, what else shall we try? If the philosophic roots of our opponents will sooner or later direct the growth of their policies toward war, should we not arrange some plan for a "preventive war" ourselves? We know there are those among us who believe this should be our course. Some of them may say that in the name of human freedom and for the sake of human progress it is our duty to do so!

Of course the answer is an unequivocal no. In the first place, the nations of the West are "peace-loving," at least in the sense that peace suits the attainments of their ends. These ends may not be always very splendid; they involve wealth, pleasure, and ease. But their attainment requires the avoidance of war. Then, too, any such program would indubitably split the western bloc of nations wide open. We could not possibly get agreement for general and joint action among them. But beneath these comparatively superficial reasons we now can understand one that lies much deeper—such a step would run counter to every principle of morality, every theory of policy that derives from our proper philosophic heritage.

Let us not underestimate the importance of this consideration. When a nation departs too far from policies based upon the traditional wellsprings of its thinking, it is apt to run into the dangers of discord. In waging a preventive war, we would not be sustained by an unquestioned conviction of the rightness of our action. Our philosophic presuppositions do not teach us that our first duty is to overcome opposition; they instill into us a wish to live and let live. The technique of total war may be forced upon us, but we should be heartsick and uneasy were we to initiate it.

Furthermore, by initiating a war we would once and for all time renounce any vestige of hope that we could become the leaders of a better world-order. We are suspect enough already for reasons, good and bad, which we have earlier partially explored. To begin a war would end forever any part the United States still plays in the dreams and hopes of man. If proof of this is wanted we need only recall the reaction of the world to our use of the first atomic bomb at Hiroshima. That action, whether or not it can be lamely defended from the viewpoint of strategy, left a legacy of hatred for the United States in much of the world. Moreover, it left a legacy of guilt upon many of us from which some of us will never quite recover. Whether we realize it or not, it did so not only because of the immediate slaughter it caused but because it was in violent discord with our deepest traditions and was completely incompatible with the principles of behavior derived from our proper philosophic sources. Any immediate advantage it won for us we are still paying for in terms of fear and insecurity. A demonstration of the awful power of the atom bomb off the coast of Japan, followed by a warning to her government that it would be used against her cities, would have served us as well in winning the war and far better for our record in the pages of history. Then too, any "preventive war" would be hailed at once by the Marxists as the fulfillment of their prophecies. They would remind the world that, according to their prophets, the rapacious capitalist nations would surely attack the socialist lands. For them it was axiomatic that this would happen and that it would be the capitalist countries that would be the aggressors. M. Thorez, the late leader of the Communists in France, in calling upon the French "proletariat" to support the Soviet Union in case of war once said: "The country of socialism cannot, *by definition,* practice a policy of aggression and war which is the deed of the imperialist powers." By definition, that is, because any such action taken by the Soviet Union *must* be in Marxist theory to defend the interests of the "workers" against their "oppressors."

In any case, one overwhelming consideration has now come into play that makes the resort to force by either side less likely although most tragically not impossible. The leaders of both the Communist and Western worlds know that no war today can be won. That should be the final "deterrent" for those among us who would so far depart from our tradition as to urge it. It should also act as such a deterrent to the Communists—no matter how intransigent their dogmas incline them to be. A general war would mean the destruction of every country and perhaps of life itself. For them too, in the philosophic sense, this should be the most powerful deterrent. For there is no sense in overcoming the "Not-self" if, in the process, the "Self" is certain also to be destroyed. Nevertheless it may unfortunately be necessary for both sides to maintain strong "deterrent forces" for a long time to come in case this ultimate realization is not faced or is temporarily forgotten.

We now come to the second of the two points we specified as those still to be discussed. Which of the two sets of philosophic foundations we have explored will give us not only the best hope of avoiding war but also best serve mankind's hope for a better future?

To a degree, we have already answered the first part of this question. We have set forth the basic reasons why the very essence of communism is combative. Its derivation from the philosophic concept of man as a creature of will and of his function as being the overcoming of opposition makes this inevitable. It should also help us to understand why communism requires the absolute subservience of the individual to the Party since it can exercise this function so much more effectively than can the individual alone. But we must now underline the reasons why our own philosophic bases provide a far better ground for the avoidance of war and for the building of a more secure world.

If man is thought of as a creature of reason and his function the understanding of his world through the greatest possible individual freedom, every step that makes peace more probable acquires additional importance, every step toward war additional hazard. For it is only in a peaceful world that our historic concept of man—and of the state—can prosper. It is interesting to note that we are so lacking in any vestige of a desire to force our will upon the world. At the end of the second World War we could easily have done just this. With our military strength at an all-time peak, with our then sole possession of the atom bomb, we could have dictated terms of settlement that would—for a time at least—have made us masters of the earth. Our defeated enemies, and indeed our Soviet ally, must have been amazed at our failure to do just this. Given such an opportunity, they would in all probability have behaved differently. Their philosophic heritage would have given them a ground for doing so. But in our heritage there is no such compulsion; this may well be the fundamental if unrealized reason why the United States did not impose its will upon the world in 1945 when the fate of the world was in its hands.

Perhaps it is not necessary to underline further the reasons why it is our philosophic bases that provide man with his best hope of a peaceful future—or of any future at all. But it still remains to point out some of the ways in which the policies proper to those bases are being either forgotten or misapplied. In addition to providing the best ground for peace and for its maintenance through discussion and reasonable compromise, our historic concept of man requires reappraisal as it is applied to the political, economic, and social problems of the world we now live in.

When that concept was first embodied in the institutions of our government, men were living in a world almost inconceivably different from ours today. Not only were our ancestors here enjoying the unprecedented advantage of having a whole continent to explore and exploit. The peoples of western Europe were spreading their control and colonization over all the earth and were sustained not only by their ability to do so because of superior arms and equipment, but also because they believed increasingly in a "mission" to civilize and Christianize the world. There seemed to be plenty of space for all, and their future looked bright indeed.

But to confine our comparisons to our own country. The United States of 1776, our nation in its first century of expansion and development, was in a very different world from that in which it lives today. It would seem unnecessary to underline that point. But there are several reasons why it is important to do so. For when we ask what our role should be in the continuing struggle that lies ahead and seek the guidelines that will best secure us, we become confused and unsure. It is easy enough to say that all we need is to make sure that we are still, in our present policies, expressing the principles that gave birth to our nation. But in our profoundly altered world this is not enough. We need not doubt the persistent strength and validity of those principles, but the times in which they were promulgated differed so much from that in which we live that they can become meaningless through misapplication if, indeed, they are not outrightly forgotten.

One outstanding example of the misapplication of principles said to be derived from our heritage is the platform developed by the group now known in our country as the Extreme Right. Those who support it claim to be the real guardians of the true traditions of the United States. They counsel withdrawal from the United Nations, diminishing or terminating all foreign aid, giving up all negotiations with the Communist world and concentration upon the "Communist menace" here at home. Their point of view appeals to young and old and is really based on a pathetic if dangerous nostalgia for a world gone by. It represents a frontier spirit in a world without frontiers. It wants to preserve or to re-create conditions that can no longer be maintained, yet its appeal is nevertheless powerful because, if those conditions *could* recur, many of the problems we face would disappear. But they cannot—isolation, self-sufficiency, security through our own armed strength belong to an age gone forever.

Most of us realize this. But we do not perhaps see what a perversion of our basic principles is here involved. Our true heritage must impel us toward full participation in the United Nations, toward maximum economic assistance, and toward continuing negotiation even in the face of frustration. It must do so because, if man is a creature of reason, all these steps are necessary to create the very possibility of peace on an overcrowded earth, now equipped with nuclear weapons of destruction. Those who oppose such steps are really turning *away* from our heritage and moving dangerously close to that of those who would put emphasis upon the concept of "overcoming opposition" as man's fundamental aim.

We should again call attention to our need to straighten out our thinking about socialism. In our inquiry we have repeatedly mentioned the need for accepting legislation often considered "socialistic" and for recognizing the need for an economy that represents a mixture of private and public enterprise. But is this not a betrayal of our philosophic heritage? Those of the Extreme Right shout loudly that it is just this. Their reaction, however, exhibits two fallacies. In the first place they cannot or will not see that the complex, populous, and polyglot nation we have become is not capable of functioning without far more governmental "interference" than was necessary when it was founded. In the second place they fail—as do so many of us—to distinguish between the sort of "democratic" socialism that plays such a large part in all the Western world on the one hand and dogmatic Marxian socialism on the other.

In every western European nation there are large active socialist parties that not infrequently gain control of the government. But there are no more implacable enemies of communism than most of their leaders, nor are any others in politics so disliked by the Communists themselves. For the democratic socialist believes with good reason that the way to prevent change by violent means is to work for the amelioration of conditions through legislation designed to improve the standard of living for the poorer members of the electorate. They are the allies and not the enemies of democracy. They are accomplishing by peaceful means a sort of mixed society in which the combined efforts of the "bourgeoisie" and the "workers" produce under a degree of governmental regulation a new social order in which all can share in the benefits. Has anyone suggested that this might be considered as the new "synthesis" in the dialectical progression, as the next step resulting from the conflict of the last hundred years? For us this may have small significance but in any case the socialists of the Western world, by their efforts to widen and secure the scope of freedom for the masses of men, are being true to the tradition of our own philosophic heritage.

If this fact could be clearly and widely recognized there would also be an end to the absurd insistence often placed upon a condition attached to our overseas aid programs—that the governments receiving such aid be "democratic" and not "socialistic." How can a new nation emerging suddenly from a state of colonial subservience or primitive ignorance take on at once the shape of the system we organized when we became a nation under such vastly different circumstances?

One very hopeful new element has been introduced into our program of overseas aid with the inauguration of our Peace Corps. The efforts of its members to live and work side by side with the peoples of the countries they assist may do a great deal to win their confidence and to increase their understanding of the principles in which the founders of our nation believed and that we at home—and abroad—all too often seem to have forgotten. Another step in the right direction is the Alliance for Progress program of aid for Latin America. Unfortunately, the stubborn resistance offered by the favored few to any change in the feudal or fascist social systems of many countries involved may prevent the success of the program.

The United States is still the world's most powerful nation. But power alone will not make or keep it the nation that has the most influence on mankind. For almost two hundred years our country has offered to mankind a realization of a dream of political freedom that has been a focus for the hope of man. In the last century we have had to compete with another dream, the one of economic security and equality that the Marxists promise to establish first by violent means and then through successive stages of their type of socialism to true communism in a classless society. We have explored the foundations of both dreams and have found that ours—with certain extensions—still provide a better support for future dreams.

The tradition of individual freedom maintained by government to the greatest degree compatible with existing conditions can and must remain our guide. We can still regard the rights of man that our Revolution affirmed as "unalienable" in a good society. But history has taught us by now that such rights mean little to men if their stomachs are empty, their backs bare, and their hearts devoid of hope. That realization must direct the policies of the United States toward creating the *conditions* of freedom both at home and abroad. We should know by now that those conditions include freedom from exploitation and that it is where this does not exist that we wage a losing battle. Our policies must always work for the establishment of those political freedoms based on our oldest traditions. In addition they must make possible not only economic opportunity but also the end of discrimination at home and exploitation abroad. We can see now that those goals were implicit in the principles we enunciated so long ago. Our measure of success in the world of tomorrow will be the degree to which we steadfastly move toward them.

In that world of tomorrow there will sooner or later emerge a new concept of man and of the sort of political and social organization best suited to his needs. Concepts based on the outdated physics of Newton—let alone the systems of Plato and Aristotle—are already beginning to provide an inadequate basis for such a concept. Perhaps a new one will gradually grow from the relativity physics of Einstein and from the new realization of the basic nature of our universe as *energy* rather than as *matter*. We are not qualified to predict the form of that new concept nor of the dream of the good society that it will engender. But we may feel secure in stating that in it the human individual will remain the focus of possible progress and that his *freedom* will therefore remain of paramount importance. For that reason it may well seem to us that no system that surrenders the prerogative of superior wisdom to the state can prevail. For that reason, too, we can feel sure that—whatever the future concept of man may be—the society he creates to meet his needs will draw more from our philosophic heritage than from any other. In it man's right to reason and to investigate and interpret his world will be sustained for the *individual* as a free inquirer and not as one directed by the state to arrive at results in accordance with dogmatic assumptions of any kind.

We have contributed much to the world of men. We shall continue to do so. But we must not be content unless all that we give in terms of material aid is complemented by what we can give in thought as well. For the world is hungry for a new dream. We can be sure that the growth of such a dream can best be nourished by our philosophic heritage.

Reading List

The Declaration of Independence, *Encyclopædia Britannica*.

The Constitution of the United States, *Encyclopædia Britannica*, cf. article on U.S.A.

The Constitution of 1936 of the U.S.S.R., *Sourcebook on European Governments*, Van Nostrand, Princeton, N.J. 1937.

Adams, Randolph G., *Political Ideas of the American Revolution*, Barnes & Noble, New York, 1958 (paper).

Aron, Raymond, *The Opium of the Intellectuals*, Doubleday & Co., New York, 1957.

Barbu, Zevedei, *Democracy and Dictatorship*, Grove Press, New York, 1956 (paper).

Bauer, Inkeles, and Kluckhohn, *How the Soviet System Works*, Vintage Books, New York, 1961 (paper).

Carew-Hunt, R. N., *Marxism, Past and Present*, Macmillan Co., New York, 1955.
Theory and Practice of Communism, Macmillan Co., New York, 1957.

Carr, E. H., *Studies in Revolution*, Macmillan Co., London, 1950.
The Soviet Impact on the Western World, Macmillan Co., New York, 1947.

Cassirer, Ernst, *The Myth of the State*, Yale University Press, New Haven, 1946 (paper, 1961).

Crossman, Richard (ed.), *The God That Failed* (Fisher, Gide, Koestler, Silone, Spender, Wright), Bantam Books, New York, 1952 (paper).

159

Daniels, Robert V., *The Nature of Communism,* Random House, New York, 1962.

Djilas, Milovan, *The New Class,* Frederick A. Praeger, New York, 1957 (paper, 1960).

Dunham, Donald, *Kremlin Target: U.S.A.,* Ives Washburn, New York, 1962.

Fichte, Johann G., *The Vocation of Man,* any standard edition.
    Addresses to the German Nation, any standard edition.

Fisher, Marguerite J., *Communist Doctrine and The Free World,* Syracuse Univ. Press, Syracuse, N. Y., 1952.

Fromm, Erich, *Marx's Concept of Man,* Frederick Ungar Pub. Co., New York, 1961.
    May Man Prevail? Doubleday Anchor Book, New York, 1961 (paper).

Goodman, Elliot R., *The Soviet Design for a World State,* Columbia Univ. Press, New York, 1960.

Hegel, G. W. F., *Philosophical History,* any standard edition.*

Hook, Sidney, *From Hegel to Marx,* Reynal & Hitchcock, New York, 1936; Ann Arbor Press, Ann Arbor, Mich., 1962 (paper).
    Marx and The Marxists, Anvil Book, Princeton, N.J., 1962 (paper).
    Documents on World Communism, Anvil Book, Princeton, N. J., 1962 (paper).

Hume, David, *Treatise of Human Nature,* any standard edition.

Koestler, Arthur, *Darkness at Noon* (novel), Macmillan Co., New York, 1941.
    The Yogi and the Commissar, Macmillan Co., New York, 1945.

Lane, Robert E., *Political Ideology,* Free Press of Glencoe, New York, 1962 (paper).

Lenin, V. I., *The Teachings of Karl Marx, State and Revolution, What Is to Be Done? (other works),* collected works of V. I. Lenin (available in pamphlet form), International Publishers, New York, 1945.

Lippmann, Walter, *Essays in the Public Philosophy,* Little, Brown & Co., Boston, 1955.
    The Communist World and Ours, Little, Brown & Co., Boston, 1959.

Locke, John, *An Essay Concerning Human Understanding,* any standard edition.

* These works may be found in Vol. III, entitled "The Political Philosophers," of *The World's Great Thinkers,* ed. by Saxe Commins and R. N. Linscott, Random House, New York, 1947.

An Essay Concerning the True Original Extent and End of Civil Government, any standard edition.*

Lukacs, John, *A History of the Cold War,* Doubleday Anchor Book, New York, 1962 (paper).

Marx, Karl, and Engels, Friedrich, *A Communist Manifesto,* any standard edition.*

Mayo, H. B., *Democracy and Marxism,* Oxford Univ. Press, New York, 1955.
An Introduction to Democratic Theory, Oxford Univ. Press, New York, 1960 (paper).
An Introduction to Marxist Theory, Oxford Univ. Press, New York, 1960 (paper).

Mehnert, Klaus, *Soviet Man and His World,* Frederick A. Praeger, New York, 1961.

Mill, John S., *On Liberty,* any standard edition.*

Miller, John G., *Origins of the American Revolution,* Little, Brown & Co., Boston, 1943.

Monnerot, Jules, *Sociology and Psychology of Communism,* Beacon Press, Boston, 1953 (paper, 1960).

Neumann, Franz, *The Democratic and Authoritarian State,* Free Press of Glencoe, New York, 1957.

Northrop, F. S. C., *The Meeting of East and West,* Macmillan Co., New York, 1946.

Padover, S. K., *World of the Founding Fathers*: *The Genius of America,* McGraw-Hill Book Co., New York, 1961.

Rossiter, Clinton, *Marxism: The View from America,* Harcourt, Brace & World, New York, 1961.

Schumpeter, Joseph A., *Capitalism, Socialism and Democracy,* Harper & Row, New York, 1950; Torchbook, 1962 (paper).

Scott, A. M., *Political Thought in America,* Holt, Rinehart & Winston, New York, 1959.

Selznick, Philip, *The Organizational Weapon,* McGraw-Hill Book Co., New York, 1952.

Somerville, John, *Soviet Philosophy,* Philosophical Library, New York, 1946.

Spitz, David, *Democracy and The Challenge of Power,* Columbia Univ. Press, New York, 1958.

Stalin, Josef, *Dialectical and Historical Materialism* (*other works*), International Publishers, New York (pamphlet).

Vyshinsky (or Vishinsky), Andrei Y., *The Law of the Soviet State,* Macmillan Co., New York, 1948.

* These works may be found in Vol. III, entitled "The Political Philosophers," of *The World's Great Thinkers,* ed. by Saxe Commins and R. N. Linscott, Random House, New York, 1947.

Wilson, Edmund, *To the Finland Station,* Harcourt, Brace & World, New York, 1940.

Windelband, Wilhelm, *History of Philosophy,* Macmillan Co., New York, 1923; Harper Torchbook, New York, 1958 (paper).

Index

Index

168 *Index*